# If Oprah Could Hear My Words

## A Journey Through
# LIFE

# If Oprah Could Hear My Words

## A Journey Through
# LIFE

Copyright © 2020 Wade F. Wilson

All rights reserved.

The characters and events portrayed in this book are fictitious. Any similarity to real persons, living or dead, is coincidental and not intended by the author.

No part of this book may be reproduced, or stored in a retrieval system, or transmitted in any form or by any means, electronic, mechanical, photocopying, recording, or otherwise, without express written permission of the author.

First Edition 2020

Cover & interior design by Nikola Baburski
Edited by Jim Martyka & Porsché Mysticque Steele
Portraits by Matt Kallish
Photography by Lavinia Aghakhani

ISBN 978-1-7361294-0-1 (Paperback)
ISBN 978-1-7361294-1-8 (e-book)
ISBN 978-1-7361294-2-5 (Hardcover)

# *Dedication*

This book is dedicated to my mother and my father whom I love very much. They have been and always will be my greatest inspiration.

# Honorable Mention

Albert William Miller, the man who gave me the confidence as a young boy to write. All it took was a moment of inspiration, a borrowed pen, a napkin, and belief.

# Table of Contents

Preface ............................................................. 1

# Chapter 1: Love ...................... 5

Con ........................................................................ 7

Love Is a One-Way Street ................................. 9

The Distance ...................................................... 11

Digital, My Fantasy ........................................... 13

Amor A Traves De Las Millas ......................... 15

Wireless, but Loved ........................................... 17

Still Dreaming of You ....................................... 19

Melt ..................................................................... 21

She Is the Color ................................................. 23

Your Guitar ........................................................ 24

Repeated Thoughts ........................................... 25

Is This Love Too? .............................................. 27

Be Mine ............................................................... 29

Long Kiss Goodbye ........................................... 31

Unreal Beauty .................................................... 33

*My Flower* ............................................................... 35

*My One. My Only. You.* ........................................ 37

*If Our Chains Were Broken* ................................ 39

*Sunshine and Moonlight* .................................... 41

*All Encompassing Love* ...................................... 43

*My Mother's Love* ............................................... 45

*Turning Point* ...................................................... 48

*Daydream* ............................................................ 50

*The Planet Behind Your Eyes* ............................ 52

*Gaea* ..................................................................... 54

*Without You* ........................................................ 55

*Real Love* ............................................................ 56

*Kiss from a Rose* ................................................. 57

*Blue Moon* ........................................................... 59

*Craving Your Curves* ......................................... 60

*Never Let You Go* ............................................... 62

*Don't Stop* ........................................................... 64

*Of Heart and Mind* ............................................. 66

*The Things I Do for Love* ................................... 68

*Puppy Love* ......................................................... 71

*Where My Heart Gets Its Color* ........................ 74

*The Proposal* ....................................................... 75

~ x ~

Defining YouMe .................................................... 76

The Greatest Love ................................................ 77

Taurus & Pisces ................................................... 79

Above My Own Depths ........................................ 81

Be Not Afraid of Love.......................................... 82

When She Looks at Me ....................................... 84

My Final Wish...................................................... 86

# Chapter 2: Heart Break ....... 87

*Lacrimam* ............................................................. 89

Simply Be Loved .................................................. 91

One + One = 1 + 1= 2............................................ 93

1 + 1= 2?............................................................... 94

1 X 1= 1. 1÷1= 1.................................................... 95

No Hope............................................................... 96

Light of 1000 Angels ........................................... 97

Cry Me a River .................................................... 99

I Lost You .......................................................... 101

Who?.................................................................. 103

The Hand Dipped in Red .................................. 105

The Things I Did ............................................... 107

Puppet ............................................................... 109

*Never Mine* .................................................. 111

*Ripped* ...................................................... 113

*My Wasted Kiss* ......................................... 114

*Book of Mine* ............................................. 116

*By the River* .............................................. 118

*Does Love Last Forever?* ........................... 120

*Haunted Heart* ........................................... 122

*Fire* ........................................................... 124

*I Thought I'd Found You* ........................... 126

*Unforgettable* ............................................ 128

*What It Means to See* ................................. 130

*Broken Love* .............................................. 132

*Stupid Cupid* ............................................. 134

*Never Cry Again* ........................................ 136

*A Man Made of Ice* .................................... 138

*Beneath These Golden Lights* ..................... 140

*Mistress* ..................................................... 142

*Trust Me* .................................................... 144

*I Am Not a Monster* ................................... 146

*I Deserve* ................................................... 149

*Giving up on Love* ..................................... 151

*Fish of Plenty* ............................................ 152

*When We Fight* .................................................................. *153*
*A Bee Without Nectar* ...................................................... *155*
*The Cheated Turned Cheater* ........................................... *157*
*Losing My First Love* ........................................................ *159*
*Beautifully Blinded* ........................................................... *161*
*Distrust* ............................................................................... *164*
*Disgust* ............................................................................... *165*
*Deserted in an Insta* .......................................................... *166*
*Holding on to Nothing* ..................................................... *168*
*Songbird* ............................................................................ *170*
*The Timid Turtle* ............................................................... *172*
*Lotus Flower* ...................................................................... *173*

# Chapter 3: Anguish ............. 175

*Flamma* ............................................................................... *177*
*The Anguish of Living* ..................................................... *179*
*An Angry Man* .................................................................. *180*
*Words Worth* ..................................................................... *182*
*Into the Dark Woods* ........................................................ *184*
*How Is It to Die?* ................................................................ *186*
*Death* .................................................................................. *189*
*Losing Brothers* ................................................................. *190*

| | |
|---|---|
| *Not Enough Tears* | 192 |
| *Withering Pride* | 194 |
| *Attempted Murder* | 196 |
| *Deceiver* | 198 |
| *My War* | 200 |
| *Without Answers* | 202 |
| *This Mad World* | 204 |
| *Death with Mortal Eyes* | 208 |
| *Lurking Shadows* | 211 |
| *Forms of Evil* | 213 |
| *Faceless* | 215 |
| *Cluttered Mind* | 216 |
| *In Memory of Butterflies* | 218 |
| *Media in White* | 221 |
| *-ism* | 224 |
| *His Hands* | 225 |
| *Addiction* | 228 |
| *A Conversation* | 230 |
| *Generation Ωmega* | 233 |
| *Fallen Stars* | 235 |
| *The Section That Night Covers* | 237 |
| *Sickness* | 239 |

*We Walk a Thin Line* ................................................... 241

*Hatred Dream* ........................................................... 244

*Beggar's Story* .......................................................... 246

*Grandfather Clock* .................................................... 250

*Blackest Book of Apathy* ............................................ 251

*My Darkness* ............................................................ 253

*It Is You I Live Through* ............................................. 254

*Reminisce a Younger Me* ........................................... 256

*Confused* ................................................................. 257

*Becoming the Comparison* ........................................ 258

*I Am My Own Worst Enemy* ...................................... 260

*Nothing* ................................................................... 262

*Over, River the Nile* .................................................. 264

*Just Another Brother* ................................................ 270

# Chapter 4: Bliss ................... 273

*Solis* ......................................................................... 275

*5MEO* ...................................................................... 277

*Women and the Happiness of Men* ........................... 278

*6-String Guitar* ......................................................... 280

*The Quest of a Passionate Flower* ............................. 282

*Reading My Book* ..................................................... 286

*Dare I Lust for Derrière* ............................................ 288
*All the World's a Stage* ............................................ 291
*Poetry* ................................................................... 293
*That's My Jam* ....................................................... 296
*Family Tree* ........................................................... 298
*Looking for Adventure* ........................................... 300
*A Supper for One* ................................................... 302
*Hiss of Snake and Letter X* ..................................... 303
*Pedal to The Metal* ................................................ 304
*A Simple Dream* .................................................... 306
*Her Hands* ............................................................ 308
*A Greater Bond* ..................................................... 311
*The Good Life* ........................................................ 315
*Rain Falls* .............................................................. 318
*Letter of Forgiveness* ............................................. 321
*Social Networking* ................................................. 325
*Master Debater of Self & Self-Pleasure* ................. 328
*Devouring Desire* .................................................. 331
*In Pursuit of Destiny* .............................................. 333
*Ability of God* ....................................................... 335
*This Present Moment* ............................................ 337
*Candid* .................................................................. 340

*Appreciate Your Real Self* ........................................... *341*

*Strand* ............................................................................ *342*

*Without a Phone* ......................................................... *343*

*Steady Drifting* ............................................................ *345*

*Slumber* ........................................................................ *347*

*Giving* ........................................................................... *348*

*Can You Stand the Rain?* ............................................ *349*

*Sunshine* ....................................................................... *350*

*Burn the Dark Clouds Away* ...................................... *351*

*Teddy Tie: A Lifelong Friend* ..................................... *353*

*Happiness Through You* .............................................. *354*

*Home Again* ................................................................. *355*

*Grateful* ........................................................................ *357*

# Chapter 5: Wisdom ............ 359

*Tertia Oculus* ................................................................ *361*

*#Black* ........................................................................... *364*

*Coppola* ........................................................................ *366*

*Courtship* ...................................................................... *367*

*The Ship of Theseus* .................................................... *368*

*Between Fear and Courage* ........................................ *369*

*We Are the Voices of Mice and Men* ....................... *371*

*Children of the Yard* ............................................. 375
*The Paradox of Imperfection and Perfection* ..... 377
*We Are in This Together* ...................................... 380
*Every Death Is a SuperNova* ................................ 381
*The Man with Many Arms* .................................. 383
*Power of Mind, Power of Us* ............................... 385
*My Future Son Asks* ............................................. 387
*Forged in Fire* ....................................................... 389
*My Gift* .................................................................. 391
*Wade's Ozymandias* ............................................. 393
*Starting Again* ...................................................... 395
*Mankind Was Given* ............................................ 397
*Conformity* ............................................................ 399
*Essence of Time* .................................................... 401
*As the Dominoes Fall* .......................................... 403
*When They Say "Impossible"* .............................. 405
*Good and Evil Illusions* ....................................... 407
*Candle Lights* ....................................................... 409
*Material Things* .................................................... 411
*The Hardest Thing to Do* .................................... 414
*Images on Fire* ...................................................... 416
*Everything Happens and There Is A Reason* ..... 417

*Destiny Is Known in Silence*.................................. *419*

*Our Digital World* ................................................ *421*

*Right Now*............................................................ *423*

*Grey* ....................................................................*424*

*Reincarnation* ....................................................*425*

*Schrödinger's Cat* ..............................................*426*

*The All* ...............................................................*427*

*Way Back* ...........................................................*428*

*The Result of Holding On* .................................*429*

*Dipped in Gold*................................................... *431*

*The Scope of Blackness* ..................................... *433*

*I Run With You*...................................................*436*

*My Poem for the World* ..................................... *440*

# About the Author............... 443

# *Preface*

Before this wonderful adventure begins, allow me to answer that burning question of yours: "Why on earth did he title his book after Oprah?" Truth be told--and I know it's cliché--it all came to me in a dream. As far back as I can remember, I grew up watching Oprah with my mom. I'm grateful for that time because although I was young and many of the topics were heavy, my mother would invite me to watch with her. As an adult looking back, I have to say it was brilliant of my mother to allow me to sit with her and watch a show that discussed all aspects of human life. My mother and I could converse for hours about an episode. This strengthened our bond, deepened our love, and secured a lifelong friendship. I was a lucky young man because where I grew up, many of my peers didn't even have a mom and technically I had two. Not only did I have a strong, influential, powerfully loving black woman whom I admired living at home. But here was this other woman of color, one of only a few positive figures I could look up to on television, and one who inspired millions. Fast forward to my college years. I had earned the nickname "Many Hats" because I wanted to be great at everything... so I tried to do everything. With each passing year, I had a new endeavor. I was all over the place, be it art, science, or business. No matter what I was doing, when my mom would call to check up on me, she'd say, "Wade...why don't you reach out to Oprah? Maybe she can help you. She's always helping folks." Being a realist, I never gave it serious thought.

In my mind, it was, "Mom, do you realize how many people inundate her email asking for help? It's a silly idea and would never ever happen to me...right?" And then, in the dream I had, it happened! This book was already written and a published work. Over time, the book made its way into Oprah's hands. She read it and she loved it. I was told that the book and other endeavors that sprang to life from this moment healed the lives of others. Upon waking, I knew in my heart of hearts I needed to make that dream a reality, even if that meant only finishing the book. We live in a world today that loves to glorify this idea of being "self-made," succeeding for yourself by yourself. I disagree. I don't believe success, no matter how big or small, is achieved alone. Everyone needs a little bit of help and sometimes all it takes is one "yes" from the right person.

The title *If Oprah Could Hear My Words* begs the question, if someone influential wanted to hear what you had to say, what would it be? If that person opened the door for you, what would you have prepared? What would you accomplish? What impact would you have in the world? After giving it much thought, I've started to take my mother's question seriously. What if Oprah could hear my words? Would anything ever come of it? The answer is, I don't know, the possibilities are endless. What I do know is that my journey begins here with all of you. I am an open book, sharing a vulnerable piece of me with a vulnerable part of you. Through this medium we are now friends, we are now kin, we are now linked. During the last episode of her talk show, Oprah said in closing, but I will say to start, "From you whose names I will never know, I learned what LOVE is."

# IF OPRAH COULD HEAR MY WORDS

CHAPTER 1 OF 5

# LOVE

THIS CHAPTER IS ABOUT LOVE.

IT IS VULNERABLE AND NAKED.

BARE AS THE FLESH.

BARING THE SOUL.

WAITING TO BE EMBRACED.

OPENED AND UNFOLDED.

IT IS ME.

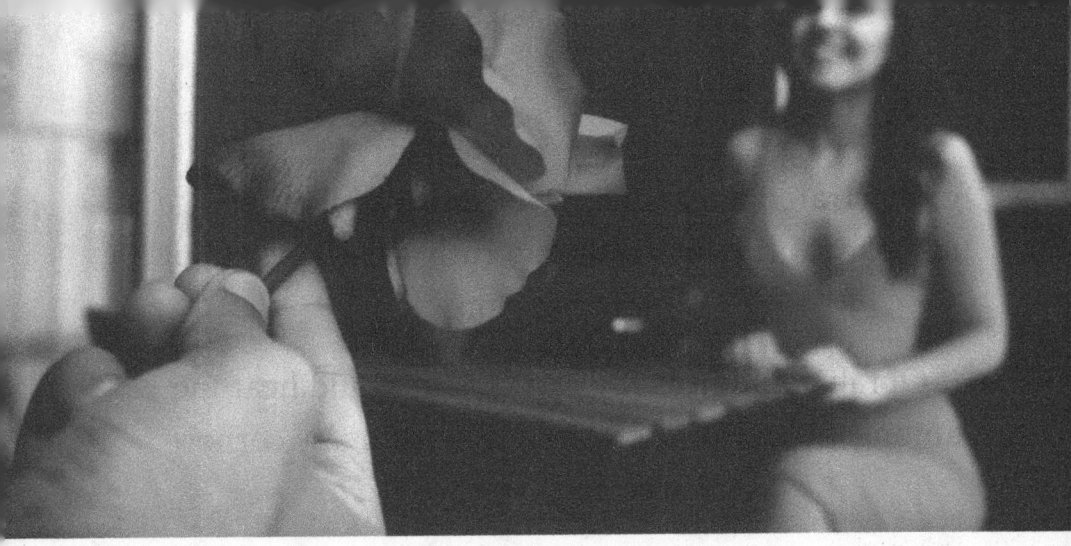

## Cor

If Oprah could hear my words, she would know I am a man written in love, written in the ways innocence is given at birth or the complexity that is the fabric of touch.

If Oprah could hear my words, she would hear a voice looking to hug the ears of those who will listen, speak to rising hearts of man, woman, and child about love and its intentions.

Phonically recite reasons as to why this profound feeling is divine in meaning.

That we seek for what we have already found, thus unknowingly continue seeking.

If Oprah could hear my words, she would know I am a man written in love.

An illustrated poem giving voice to a soul otherwise unspoken, bringing forth my truth self-silenced but now chosen.

If Oprah could hear my words, she would hear me amongst the waves, crashing against every corner, crevice and concave.

Rippling out and bonding one instant or the smallest measurement of time, so small, we've missed it.

If Oprah could hear my words, she would know we carry identical names, we are all pieces of illustrated poetry and we are all beautifully framed.

It is what ties us to everything, I believe it is our fate.

We are all love, we are the same, we are the human race.

*Chapter 1: Love*

# *Love Is a One-Way Street*

Who said pain is love and love is pain? Because I must protest this, love does not understand pain & pain knows not what love is.

Love is a one-way street and the direction it moves is pure and sweet.

Like rushing rapids, I smile while caught in its tide, the feeling, the sensations beyond what I can describe, but still I try.

It's pleasure uplifting, splendor sending, everything on a destination down a one-way street. Hearts in romance, rhythmic to harmonious beat, when pain arrives, it's the lover who drifted off onto the wrong road I speak.

The lovers who choose to jump on the downward spiral, will wallow in sorrow and point blame at crimson red.

However, love is a one-way street and only tried giving direction for the lovers to find their way back to their feet.

So, you see, to live in love is to take part in the divine, pain can only be invited, it's not yours or mine.

So, who said pain is love and love is pain?

Because I must protest this, love does not understand pain & pain knows not what love is.

Love is a one-way street and it's on this path we are free.

# The Distance

In my mind, your presence lingers.

When I rest these dreary eyes, I hold fast to memories that tickle my heart and ease the soul at night.

I count each heartbeat as they stir images of our moments together into dreams.

In the distance I reach, hoping you are somewhere reaching back.

In the distance I stare, wishing to see you, wishing you could see me too.

When I stand alone, I imagine you here with me.

When I listen to the seas, I swear it is you speaking to me.

Into the distance I yell, my feelings taking to currents like tidal waves.

Leaving me behind to wonder; did they receive them?

Did my calling ever crash against their shore and will I ever have more?

I awake tomorrow only for the chance I may have to see you.

Looking into the distance, our future I may not know.

However, with you, I am willing, no matter how far we may go.

With these hands I support the legs of a broken bridge, waiting for the moment you walk across it.

Anxiously anticipating the chance of release.

Time is of the essence and the time we have is short. I grasp every second and treasure them into my chest, I treasure them deep, before being flung back into the distance.

Flung from gentle kiss and passions that bring me to life.

So, embrace me now, take this moment and make it ours.

Mystical memories that can be felt in the distance, seen in the distance, heard in the distance.

Through distance of time, distance of thought and distance of space.

Feel our love beating, calculating the sum, welding the distance between us, until the time we can finally be one.

*Chapter 1: Love*

# *Digital, My Fantasy*

Once upon a time through the internet, two souls found each other and then connected.

It started off as play, an online crush from far away.

But something shined through, so strong, we could feel it.

I passed off my heart through seven single digits.

Not long after, my phone rang.

When I heard her voice, my heart sang.

She didn't know I knew, but it had to be, the woman on the other line I wanted madly.

Our bond is thick, like the base of a tree and every leaf is an extension of how our love is free.

I never questioned how we bonded so perfectly.

Although she's the digital love I can't have solely.

I say; she is my dream come true, a lady with all I want, so I'll keep on wanting you.

In my dreams, I imagine her lying with me, however the woman I am falling for is still just something I fancy.

Through digital love, all I can say is; I hope one day we are more than just a depiction.

That I am your man to be, based on fact and we can rewrite this fiction.

Sure, we dial up and connect, however, I wish to make us a reality.

Forming pixels into whole pictures, outside of this digital fantasy.

Chapter 1: Love

# Amor A Traves De Las Millas

Nos conocimos en el campo de batalla, we met on the battlefield.

Brutal as it was beautiful, they are the ones I decided to die with.

They are the final bullet pressed into chamber and fired; they are the final cry of hope for love across the miles.

Separados por el fuego, I survive to see them.

Hay una frontera entre nosotros, I rally against the odds to cross it.

A witness to tragedy, the warzone understands my bloodshed.

Through smoke and burning flesh, I hear "toma mi mano" and we go.

Juntos tomamos un salto de fe, from the highest building we fall, sealing our bond.

They would revive a fallen soul, healing a wounded heart the way only a medic could.

As bombs burst and screams rise, I pray they feel my love across the miles.

Two factions, two bulls going head to head.

No tenemos idea de como va a terminar.

However, despite the darkness and mystery ahead, y seguimos adelante de todos modos.

We are love across the miles, Amor A Traves De Las Millas.

*Chapter 1: Love*

# Wireless, but Loved

Through tides and what binds us deep, love seems to be out of farthest reach.

Like gravity, my heart pulls love from the sky and thus I found it, without not seeing why.

I don't understand, but it feels so familiar, like I've known it all my life played out in the theater.

Vibrant and live, this feeling is so chilling.

I imagine sharing the stage with her, it is passion…thus living.

I could dream, but it fails to compare.

Wireless connection, I breathe seduction through air.

I can only imagine her touch and spend unconscious time imagining as much.

Subtle kiss, she tastes of honey, sweet in entirety, her body is beyond lovely.

Cursed miles between us, only shortened by electricity.

whom remains unforgiving, uncaring and without sympathy.

Just a voice, or pixels by image, not having you is cause for my grimace.

I am your prince, you my princess.

Bound by immortal fate, time has been our witness, that through lifetimes boundless of reach, infinite space or specs of sand silenced on a beach, somehow, someway, we will reunite.

Because romantic passion as pure as ours, through history and future, will forever ignite.

Chapter 1: Love

# Still Dreaming of You

I am sitting here thinking, daydreaming, but something keeps invading and clouding my thoughts.

My surroundings are hazed, my mind in a daze, but soon there in front of me, is you.

Time flying without signs of stopping, days passing and still I dream of you.

These dreams consume my life at night, these dreams consume my life in sun.

The only time they consume not, is when you and I can have fun.

My body is constantly clawing and craving to get near you.

Worrying when you're away, dreading the angst I'll be feeling.

I am like a dog at the door, wondering where you are, pondering what you are doing and barking aloud for your return.

As long as you're gone you will be my desire.

Dreams without meaning unless the meaning is you.

Understand, this reality of mine is truly this love inside.

You are my life, my love and my fairy tale.

Every moment I spend in absence, I am still dreaming of you and to tell you the truth...I love every second of it.

Where there would be emptiness, I am fulfilled.

Fulfilled in a world of dreams I am always having of you.

Chapter 1: Love

# *Melt*

Why is it when I see you, I seem to melt?

You move and I shiver, biting bottom lip in tribute to your bottom motion.

A shock to the system like a freezing dive into the ocean.

If I had to run laps forever, you always out in front, would be my life's greatest motivation.

Hell, simply speaking your name feels like I've swallowed capsaicin.

...Hot.

Why is it when you talk, I smile and listen?

Lost in every subtle note, the sound of your voice is my favorite melody to hear.

You're my Pied Piper and the tune you play impulses me to immediately fall onto one knee and pledge my devotion.

Hell, I can't play a single game without you, I need you, you are my token.

Why is it when I'm mad, you exhale and the anger inside me escapes?

Leaving me clear, giving me hope in the sense we are inexorable and although I love it, how dare you make me feel this vulnerable.

Why is it when you glide past me, my nose tingles from the scent of blossoms in bloom?

I am the bee to your flower's pollen, milk and honey too.

I believe you help me see the truth between the religious and the atheist, a spiritual and scientific fact called love, a truth known throughout the ages.

Why is it when my days seem dark, your eyes brighten it?

From glow in iris, one man's view in self-singularity broadens.

This apple becomes ripe and reverts from being rotten.

I may stand from afar, but I see all I need to see to know that you are the night sky filled with stars.

Gorgeousness, an unparalleled beauty above me.

I know what love lay in my heart, what I feel is tangible.

In dreams and in present I want you, so tell me...why is it whenever I try to get close to you, all I do is melt?

*Chapter 1: Love*

# *She Is the Color*

Red.

She is the color red.

Passionate & strong, she is my morning sun.

She is glorious & there's nothing left to be said.

Until I raise my white flag, she will always be my color.

Red.

# Your Guitar

I am your curves to hold and I am your strings to touch.

Tease me and I'll hum, play me and I'll sing.

Alone I am mute, together we are instrumental.

In solitude I am dust, but with you, our love is music.

Chapter 1: Love

# *Repeated Thoughts*

A broken record plays in my head from repeating words and thoughts burned into my heart.

My feelings for you are twisted on the hands of a clock infinitely moving, but always resetting the day.

These repeated thoughts fill an already crowded mind, feeding on thoughts inferior to dreams of missing my lover.

These repeated thoughts move in the sideways eight of infinity's shape, looping itself into this never-ending cycle of repeated thoughts.

Could I have finally found a love that cannot be dismembered into two separate halves?

Have I finally found a love that, like my dreams, can last forever?

Could our love exist in a place beyond the heavens not bound by space and forged time?

I ask these questions because my thoughts repeatedly ask me.

I'm in love, you see.

Thus, you are my repeated thought and I hope our love is repeated throughout history because you are now my only thought, the only thought for me.

*Chapter 1: Love*

# Is This Love Too?

I am unsure.

Could I be fooled by my heart, desperation forming love with what I conspire, connecting the bridges between pillars of man and woman?

What be these signs I see or am seeking?

How can I, meek and mild, be so sure in asserting beating organ outwardly, when love can be one-sided and blind?

Feelings that I feel enriched with sweet taste of wine, intoxicating, might be a drunken stupor that I alone ferment in.

Needless to say, I rejoice in this sensation.

Part of me willing to go to my grave, holding tightly to a thought I wish not to share, for truth of answer may be too much to bear.

Cruel this purgatory, a lifetime spent in regret.

Wandering while wondering and pondering; what could have been next?

Tease of smile then sketches across my lips, I tickle inside as I am reminded how they make me happy.

Everything they do and everything they say…it takes me.

However, here I am okay, here, in this embrace.

Because love can play tricks, it can play a painful game.

But whatever the answer, at least I know this.

Prior to speaking out and letting my inner depths be known, I take comfort here, in this time before, for this too is love.

# Be Mine

There are no words to describe this pattern, this beautiful design.

I believe we refer to God when we encounter the divine.

Unexplained, the reasoning is beyond self.

My words too feeble in attempt to express this feeling of worth, therefore I've remained silent as my heart bursts through sealed walls.

Please forgive me as I try to find the meaning of deliverance when in the presence of your love.

All was still as portrait when eyes first laid upon thee.

Eyes remained captured to iris as heart fluttered in memory.

Although distant in touch, I was thankful as much, for God put you in the essence of my light.

Dare I wish, that you in Lord's majesty, take unworthy hand and waltz.

Waltz with me through this dream and journey far upstream, where we both can sing free.

I've been asleep and for you I will wake from a coma, if thee accepts humble hand in promise. Beauty, I say this.

Me, the real me, will be thy one true and faithful kiss.

Upon adventurers return, take chance and leap.

Fall into my arms and see if soft enough to sleep and if so...know.

I will hold on close through this dreamer's dream, for you are fantasy.

## Chapter 1: Love

# Long Kiss Goodbye

Lips ignite, as hidden passion reveals itself.

Flames dance, clearing trees, which kept this love a secret.

As pine burns, the yearning for the other intensifies.

Thick clouds of white smoke lift our souls to peak the highest mountain and still with miles to experience.

However, strong winds will blow us apart.

I know not for how long, nor the count of days, but I do know our long kiss goodbye will speak in my dreams until our lips connect again.

Fire hot, sent cold chills up my spine.

Body relaxed, I fell into an ocean topped with roses.

A long kiss goodbye renewed life again.

What was forgotten was found, it is realized through you.

Now, put your arms around me, kiss these tender lips and feel my heart against yours.

Lose yourself in this world we've created, make this moment last forever, make every second echo and sing of a long kiss goodbye.

Separate paths split us into halves therefore, take hold to endless love and pull towards the center.

A long kiss goodbye will be a gateway to something only love can give.

With one kiss, one touch, a rose can blossom and love will flourish...and so, I toast.

To a long kiss goodbye and what lies ahead of you and I, for an ending only arises after something profound has begun.

Chapter 1: Love

# *Unreal Beauty*

Unreal beauty does exist.

Branded into the eyes of the beholder, she is an angel born from the fountain of youth.

I feel young in her wake, behold, she is the bearer of unreal beauty.

Never fading, she endures the ever-testing realities of life.

She is beautiful, in all ways, not just one.

I love her now and I'll love her in future.

Growing old, I will love her then.

As I wither and shrivel, she'll remain perfect, her spirit more precious than gold.

A gift from God, acquired only by a Goddess.

I am awed in the morning when she rises, and I am awed by her when she sleeps.

I love her when she's happy, I even love her when she weeps.

I'll love her at her best and I'll love her at her worst.

Unconditional and forgiving, her beauty is unreal to me.

Perhaps it's because the way I feel or maybe it's because I behold the eyes?

Either way, I love her deeply and uniquely we make a pair.

The world is just the two of us, open and free and she will continue to be an unreal beauty to me.

*Chapter 1: Love*

# My Flower

Snow smothering a rose out in the cold, frail and dying, I pick its delicate petals from the ice.

In my cupped hands, I warm it with bodily heat, care for it with green thumb, until beautiful flower returns vibrant with color, fulfilling life with scent and pleasant abundance.

My flower, center of joy, whom I'd be not without.

Wilts until I smile and darkens until I laugh.

When such essence leaves and weariness overtakes, I pour from amour, purist of waters until radiant at core, till roots soak what brilliance I adore.

My flower, deserving of angelic butterflies.

Forever will I keep you close to my heart, beating such soft life from me to you, regardless of what may come our way.

I am lucky to have found you, you are my flower, this I am proud to declare.

Relishing every minute of every moment on our journey.

Enjoying the touch during long summer nights yet simmer still as we sizzle under radiant daylight.

My flower, we shall grow together as one.

My flower, my beloved for a lifetime.

Chapter 1: Love

# *My One. My Only. You.*

My one. My only. You.

One of a kind, free and dancing about.
Untamed, she is wild and unkempt, like a unicorn on the Great Plains.

My one. My only. You.

I step into foreign lands in search for what is rare, as tides move the Earth, releasing love from cocoon.

My one. My only. You.

Time has led me so quickly to your heart, the only ones of our kind together within loving truth strung from harp.

My one. My only. You.

Just for a moment, even a part of time, we can awaken what lies inside, remembering that we deserve the best and we are best together.

My one. My only. You.

Happiness comes and goes, but ours would last a lifetime.

Whether hands conjoin or passionate eyes remain the primary contact, for a moment in time, even just a second, I know you will always be-

My one. My only. You.

Chapter 1: Love

# *If Our Chains Were Broken*

If our chains were broken, how would I react?

What would happen to my feelings, where would I be at?

I hate to think of such things, true love wasted on precious time, time lived only once and only worth its riches if you remain mine.

If our chains were broken, what on Earth would I do?

Could I survive a rip that cannot be mended by glue?

How could I live on a puzzle built in riddle?

A puzzle without the one piece to fill the empty middle.

I'd be a man with a missing heart, a mind without a soul, a shadow in tears and a star in the dark on its own.

If our chains were broken; may God forbid, I may slip into silence and lose the will to live.

I'd rather sleep at peace under this dream, than to give into your absence ended in nightmarish scream.

But, why do I waste in this thought?

Pretending as if my artery has already suffered blood clot, when you are the clasp holding the chain together.

I show its beauty as I wear it, for I am love's bearer.

I keep you close, always where you mean the most to me and I yell to the world of your angelic greatness boastfully.

This chain we share is my one keepsake, I grasp one end and the other you take.

We pull towards the center until met as one ring and our chain becomes unbreakable as heaven sings.

If our chain were broken; I laugh, for that could never be.

Our love is much too strong, a chain which is forever binding.

*Chapter 1: Love*

# Sunshine and Moonlight

I remember when I saw you, you lit up the sky.

Radiance so bright, your image burned into my eyes.

Days were sunny, your warmth kept the skies clear.

I knew then, I always needed you near.

Is this the cure to my heartache and misery?

A God send, therefore a heavenly delivery?

I wake in the morning to my beautiful sunshine and sleep at night comforted by gentle moonlight.

When the colors fall, you illuminate the dark.

Stars shimmer and the moon's blue glow glistens.

Even in the faintest night, through you, I can see the way.

Through you, twilight is the time of dreams.

Can you see it?

Fireflies dance around us as we kiss.

They are thousands and thousands of cherubs, coming to celebrate two angels and the engagement of true love's bliss.

Yawning, I wake in the morning, longing to see my sunshine burst above the horizon.

Only later to rest, thankful to see her eyes and the heavens within.

Moonlight perfect, you pull me away from cursed sin.

You are my sunshine and you are my moonlight.

You are my warmth and my cozy bed.

Time goes by and by and I know you will remain in my sky.

For, what is worth waking up, if I can't awake to my beautiful sunshine?

What night is worth sleeping under, if I can't be calmed by my moonlight?

I remember when I first saw you, you lit up my sky.

What was true then is true now even though many years have passed by.

You are my sunshine and you are my moonlight.

You are my entire sky.

## *All Encompassing Love*

Love...into which encompasses all things.

Complex is its shape, simple in how it's used.

Difficult to see, yet so easy to feel.

Love...into which encompasses all things.

Understand first, that love is blind.

Love is void of form, but love is free.

In love, color exists none, for without eyes, it cannot see.

In love, judgment does not hold, for love has no shape to reference, nor object to perceive.

But love in its eternal grace wanders free amongst the energies of you and me.

Love...bonds of life forever holding.

Love...placed into delicate creation.

Love...its properties known in smile; its properties known in kiss.

Love...into which encompasses all things, into which all things are born...

# We are... love.

Chapter 1: Love

# My Mother's Love

Mom.

I want to say I love you, because I know I don't say it enough.

I want to say thank you, because I know you've been taken for granted.

I often think how unfair it is, that the greatest gift I will ever know is my mother's love.

That from the moment I arrived from womb, the only other love more profound would be of God itself.

I have rattled my brain and stretched it to the limit.

Meditated and met with divine spirits.

Even went as far as developing and solving an equation in modern physics just to figure out how I can repay you for all that you've done.

But, as I get older, with clarity, I see there is none.

So, mom, I want to say I love you.

You deserve at least that much.

I want to say; thank you, though I know it's not enough.

I am wise beyond my years because of the knowledge bestowed by you.

I am loving, kind and compassionate because your actions were my view.

You helped me see that in a world of I, there is truly only we.

Everything that I am; in honor of you, I grew up to be.

I am reminded of this precious gift called life whenever I look into a mirror.

Through the reflection of you, what could be haze is now clearer.

Mom.

You helped paint my dreams and embrace my tears.

Fueled me with ambition and kept me going despite my fears.

With nurturing love, unconditional and selfless, like a flower, I prospered and today I flourish. Mom.

I want to say I love you; I hope I have made you proud.

I want to say thank you; your grace has left me at times speechless and wowed.

*Chapter 1: Love*

Your son is one of the luckiest men on Earth. Lucky because my stars aligned at birth. Yes, there is no love quite like a mother's love and so I'll end with…mom, I love you. Thank you.

Dedicated to

~ My Mom

# Turning Point

We were friends from the start, we said friends to the end.

We shall not fight, leave each other's side nor ever say goodbye to one another and then there came the

turning point <> *tniop gninrut*.

Friends through school, friends at parks, friends at parties and friends at home.

We said friends forever, abbreviated as BFF's and then there came the

turning point <> *tniop gninrut*.

Laughter, screams and tears of joy.

You go your way and I'll go mine.

Halls become unfamiliar, youthful echoes are now faint.

Adulthood calls without choice as we follow our fate and then there came the

turning point <> *tniop gninrut*.

We said friends forever, I dearly hope it will be.

You'll be there and I'll be here, hoping we keep the path open and clear and then there came the

turning point <> *tniop gninrut.*

But fret not, I say this; when we say goodbye, our goodbyes aren't forever, a day, or years.

"Why" you may ask?

Because we said friends forever, forever turning back on our

tniop gninrut <> *turning point.*

# Daydream

I stand here before you, my heart indeed is racing.

Inside my mind countless thoughts and feelings are pacing.

I can't figure out if this is real or just a fantasy.

My Piscean eyes can only see this romantically.

It yearns frantically for two oceans to collide dramatically, altering the reality of theatre and dance.

But we are not a show, we are merely a burning sun's glance.

In this daydream, we fear life and love's end.

But when in your embrace, life and love we do extend.

Time has not passed, during this day that I dream, the sands have stopped flowing through my hourglass.

Maybe I am a fool for starting to fall for a dream?

But it seems this fall was fate, igniting this unspeakable fire all out of one date.

Daydream...daydream...she is truly a daydream.

Her touch still lingers long into the night.

## Chapter 1: Love

I felt love's pain and now she's become my light.

Whether this is fictional or real, she connected to my soul and it's her magnificence I deeply feel.

If my iris must remain covered by lids, I thank God for daydream's kiss and one cupid's arrow that did not miss.

# The Planet Behind Your Eyes

We are an inquisitive bunch.

Exploration is our ship and curiosity our current.

Questions be asked, answers be sought, and meaning be found.

However, the world is not enough.

Stars freckle the wondrous face of night and we are compelled to discover its mysteries.

To the moon, to Mars and beyond our legacy will venture out.

But not I.

I am fine right here beside you.

The universe is largely unknown but I have found an affinity for exploring your infinity and should my world ever collapse, it's to the planet behind your eyes, I'll go.

The most unique and beautiful place I've always called home.

Born for adventure and birthed to brave the wild, it is our nature to fear but delve further into the unknown.

*Chapter 1: Love*

So here I am on a rocket with honest tremble about the future, happiest discovering more of you.

All of you and the beautiful person you are.

# Gaea

Earth goddess.

Beautiful as you are, I pick the flowers you leave in your wake.

No matter how far.

As you go, I'll go, and so, we will always go together.

Chapter 1: Love

# *Without You*

Every day I wake up, I look forward to seeing you.

Your presence blushes my skin until I am completely see through.

Even right now, I know I am completely transparent.

That way you see my truth and can believe I present myself without arrogance.

I'm just a schoolboy, giddy with a young crush.

I try to fight it but gave up because I love you so damn much.

The hardest part of the day is watching stars consume blue, because when my day ends, it's hard to be without you.

# Real Love

I know I am in love; I know what I feel is real love because nothing can substitute this heavenly, pure, light-weighted emotion that only God's angel could show me.

I am always overjoyed when I am embraced by your wings; life seems so much more enriched whenever we are together realizing our real love.

I wish to have you so in my life; my love is eternally a gift that I wish to give to you, a gift I wish to deliver to an angel from God's Eden.

What I feel is real love and you are my entrance to a place everyone strives to gain acceptance to; blessed paradise and true ecstasy.

Strip me of my sins and let us begin our lives together, enjoying our happiness behind heaven's gate as one with our real love.

# Kiss from a Rose

They say the sweetest things in life come from mother nature.

That the sweetest things in life are natural and pure.

Like a kiss from a rose's red velvet lips.

Coursing nectar in passionate touch of mouth, unspoken and expressing fiery tales of thought falling in the Ides of March.

Spring forth, I now blossoming in undeniable truth.

I have been kissed by a rose.

Befuddled by bubbling brooks of bounty.

Riches upon riches in wealth seeping from pores.

As if poisoned, see sweat brimming upon brow.

I am bleeding, gently pricked by thorns from embraced stem.

I am bitten and now stricken with longing.

A kiss from a rose's red velvet lips.

Soft petals caressing the tickle of my pallet.

I taste in orgasm the pleasure of knowing nothing more innocent.

They say the sweetest things in life come from mother nature.

That the sweetest things in life are natural and pure.

Like being kissed by a rose, thereby making the sweetest thing in life...you.

*Chapter 1: Love*

# Blue Moon

Summertime is warm, the moon is pretty blue.

Your hugs are warmer, I love to hold you.

The moon's true beauty, it cannot compare.

You are stunning with glare, you are divine, you are rare.

The light from sun guides me through days, but the light you give me, guides me to your arms in many ways.

The moon is wonderful where it is placed.

With all the stars glimmering around its pretty blue face.

Your eyes are those twinkles and your depth is beyond the knowing of place and I am a lowly astronaut lost in the vastness of your space.

Wintertime is cold, the moon is pretty new and although new the year, for many a blue moon, I will always love you.

# Craving Your Curves

My mouth waters at the thought of your curves, exhilarating my heartbeat till flexing of nerves.

Can I say that your bountiful body is beauty beyond its bounds, worthy of worship and marvel of its radiance so profound?

Gander I must at a gorgeous bust, my mouth moistens at the mere thought of exploring blessed bumps.

I wish to climb to the top of two hills with my gentle lips and fall deep between the crevice, hitting land with sensational kiss.

Lay down as I praise your monuments that rise, feel as I begin devouring your delicious desert held secret by delectable thighs.

I will even love your asset, disowned by a life of always being the rear, I'll worship your posterior and savor it without fear.

To your body I gravitate like a moth to a bulb, nothing else can satisfy until it is you I hold.

## Chapter 1: Love

Your beauty is like the sun bringing a type of light into my life, you have given this blind man the magnificence of sight.

Irresistible and forever tempting, I am craving your curves.

A pirate thinking of that bounty, baby it is you I urge; let me play on you like a water ride, my tongue can be the slip and your body can be the slide.

I'll worship you, the sensuous curve of my delight, a delicacy so tender, I want…no!

I crave to bite.

# Never Let You Go

What do you get when we are put together?
I could tell you, but you may not want to hear that.

I try to find an obvious connection, bringing stars to the universe so we can see it in its splendor, swim freely in its vast oceans and not once speak of its existence, however, always know it's there.

I heard spoken through supple lips, "I never want to let you go."

Always stepping in my heart were feelings, "I will hold on and keep you close."

Never will I let you go, these words felt by us mutually, hinting passion of a word dwelling in us both, a word in which I can only express my feelings, yet, a word that remains a ghost.

I covered deserts with flowers so we can admire its beauty, breath in deeply, fill our hearts completely and not once speak of its existence, however, always know it's there.

What do you get when we are put together?
I could tell you, but you may not want to hear that.

*Chapter 1: Love*

While we remain quiet, our hearts scream in defiance at our silence of this word we dare not speak, while our souls hold on to each other, pleading, "Never will I let you go!"

Persistently getting closer, even after being pushed away, but you brought me back and I know where I want to stay.

I placed stars in the universe and flowers in the deserts so we can see the word we dare not say, so we know even without it, love exists with us anyway.

# Don't Stop

When I lay you on my bed and approach, will you stop me as clouds conform to vivacious curves and prideful rock laying upon gentle stream?

When I run my strong hands up along your smooth thighs, will you stop me as the trees rise on tender flesh and Earth trembles under supple breast?

When I pull off your undergarments and your legs become inviting, will you stop me as the soul yearns enticing love, calling for touch, wanting of needing, filling the air with your sweet aroma, arousing my temptations of teasing?

When I kiss your lips, sweet and tender like plums, as the nape of your neck swells and the passion fruit of youth begins oozing us, primal in nature, essential to life, stimulating elements enthralled, flowing of hastened blood now moving through my body, bringing golden key to crystal lock, I ask...will you stop me?

When I enter into love and it hurts, will you stop me as your gentle hands clench to heavy back and dreamy eyes set to gaze stars?

*Chapter 1: Love*

When whispered words of mine and whispered words of love are spoken, when I push the key a little deeper and your womanly miracle opens, will you stop me?

Now together, we breathe and sensitivity increases, emotions pure, hidden deep, in an instance releases, the motion in sync and the passion intense and still I wonder, when the Earth moves violently and all seems as though it will shake apart, will you stop me?

When you take my hand and squeeze it firmly, will you stop me?

When time has elapsed and I gently pull away...tell me, will you stop me? Or will you pull me back and say, "baby, don't stop!"

## *Of Heart and Mind*

You are my everything, you are my world!

I've always wondered the meaning and then you gave my heart a twirl.

These phrases are cute, they convey a lot of emotion.

Whilst in the throes of romance, I must unpack these words before spoken.

You are my everything!
It is the most accurate story I can tell.

A wayward vagabond, finding refuge within your conch shell.

I was birthed long ago but didn't live until the grace of you.

If my life was then predetermined, you were the redo.

When I say you are my everything, I'm saying you are my mind.

every thought, every dream, you are the entity of design.

## Chapter 1: Love

Therefore, you are my world, from whom I derive feeling.

The rhythmic symphony, from whom provides biblical healing.

When I say you are my world, I'm saying you are my heart.

The energetic flow, the clock to me, life can now impart.

You are my world; you are my everything!

You are the all-in prayer I am worshipping.

You are of my heart and you are of my mind.

You are the infinity I have longed to find.

# The Things I Do for Love

I could be Romeo, romantic as Shakespeare, weave all words into a basket of beauty if that's what you want to hear.

Say roses are red and violets are blue, love is like a Disney fairy tale; but you and I both know that's not true.

It takes more than emotion and repetition of undying devotion.

Deeper still, it takes more than magic spells and mystical potions.

I preach, love is something we open.

Yet, how can we share this treasure from the box, when it's the box we have no hope in?

In the name of love, I decree; I will take care of <u>me</u> for <u>you</u>, if <u>you</u> take care of <u>you</u> for <u>me</u>.

The greatest gift a person could give, complete awareness of self and from consciousness live. From my view, the sins I harbor should not be a burden you bear, it is my armor and my weight to wear.

## Chapter 1: Love

Further, I recognize you carry your own, so to love you is not to pelt you with my many pebbles, rocks and stones.

Nor will I enable, certain promises are unnatural and unloving.

If I gave you the world, what would you have left to gain?

Wouldn't our love then decompose and ferment into something you and I could no longer maintain.

I imagine it would, but it doesn't have to be like that.

You can be my hero, but I can scratch my own back.

I accept that you're not flawless, I also trust you'll make good on your flaws; yes?

I promise I'll make good on mine, combined, we define progress.

Understanding that anything human is not alien to me, so why pretend?

There's no reason to fight you, when I am the only one, I should contend with.

Self-development and the lifelong pursuit of wisdom, we create a united empire by strengthening our own individual kingdoms.

Despite popular belief, love is conditional and true love respects those conditions, the obvious and subliminal.

Two can truly love when they see self-matters, I believe it is the key to fairy tale endings and happily ever afters.

We are all caterpillars pupating in chrysalis and before we flutter, only we can utter what type of butterfly we'll be.

So, I say to thee, these are the things I do for love, the things I do for <u>you</u> & <u>me</u>.

Chapter 1: Love

# *Puppy Love*

Everybody talks about puppy love; you know the type; it's so cute it's going to make me sick kind of puppy love.

Butterfly and Eskimo kisses, they're so wrapped up in each other; the world could end, and both would miss it.

Note, this is not coming from a bachelor's or bachelorette's perspective.

I say this without jealousy or intent to be harmfully negative.

Truth is, I too share in the splendor of having a significant other.

My relationship maybe old, but I reminisce of a time when it was younger.

Two people, one life, hearts racing every day in excitement without strife.

Cheeks blush, eyes widen, there was nothing more beautiful than us.

Don't get me wrong, it hasn't lost its luster; but when people speak about relationships, they talk about the sweet and forget about the sour.

Yes, love can be bitter...the question is, how do you deal?

Something I didn't understand because nobody talks about when things get real.

Like that one night...when the sex wasn't good.

Or our first fight, I mean, how many times are they going to get "put the dishes away" misunderstood?

They even farted in their sleep; I didn't know my lover could stink; but then again, how many times have I held it in until the brink?

And hey; I'm with you, love is a wonderful feeling, I only wish I was aware it evolved.

As the days accumulated, I became naturally comfortable with whom I was involved.

Our annoying habits revealed themselves, imperfections busting out.

But you know what?

It's crazy, our puppy grew up and we still loved it with zero doubt.

## Chapter 1: Love

Yes, fairy tales are shallow, the beginning is all about impressing; but when things get real, you learn to love that salad with or without the dressing.

You've heard it before that love is unconditional.

In other words, I will love my partner in any and all conditions.

Young and naïve, I didn't comprehend the depths of that statement.

When you declare someone as your partner, that is the beginning of a lifelong engagement.

Some would say there is nothing better than puppy love and I would respectfully disagree; puppy love is fun, but only up until a certain degree.

Because when love becomes cold and it's harder to feel, it takes that grown wolf kind of love to stay around, when things get real.

# Where My Heart Gets Its Color

Her eyes are like a prism, and in their reflection the beauty of the world can be seen.

She is the spectrum, bending light into color and I, a simple canvas caught within her gaze.

My melancholy monochrome becomes a gradient of more than absolute blacks and whites.

It's brimming with life, she is a painter, master of oils and pastels and the rays amongst mist.

Arching rainbows between us, bridging the bland and the brilliant, she is the colors of my heart and promise.

*Chapter 1: Love*

# *The Proposal*

Faintest quiver set upon lips as I seek fleeting will to place halo as ornament around the neck of palm's arm.

Am I of morning coward, yellow-leafed as dew permeates from crest, fruitless in attempt, whilst doting upon poetry to bear ripe fruit?

On this day, I pray thine gives ear to such undeserved.

Permitting beggar to humble before his majesty, anchored down by weighted limb arching like mountain peaks.

Hath eyes ever gazed clearer once in thy presence?

Forgive emphatic tribute of love for this force impinged upon me.

Hither I am still, exhibiting truth from seed heaven doth consent, thou art mine and only heart in flesh.

Thus, I fain braving hand toward thee from inner depths. I cling to this feeling I try to describe with feeble words.

Hark as I proclaim!

Marry me!

*A Journey Through LIFE*

# *Defining YouMe*

In my life, no one will be you.

In your life, no one will be me and, in this universe, during this time; no one combination will be us.

So, YouMe together, is the rarest, everything forever.

It is the most divine place I'll ever know.

# The Greatest Love

I have found I was a broken man.

Lost in a world of lust, beaten by heartbreak and distantly lost.

Cooled by the frost in temperatures of despair, gasping for air, I was left wishing for love in desperate prayer.

Tears long polluted, rained from eyes like the Ganges.

My woe potential sustenance for alluring succubus and wild banshees.

But these tears in miracle, fell upward with grace, away from temptation and this heathenness place.

Meanwhile, below, I continued my search, only to find more lies, why's and denial.

Dark clouds now tainted what was once a sunny soul, but when all hope was given up, an angel appeared upon a grassy knoll.

Not with intent to end me, she sprouted tulips, roses and sunflowers so vibrant with color, time at this moment existed without hours.

My eyes squinting in fear of viewing something so radiant, I doubted this gift and my nobility of obtaining it.

Resenting such perfection, I wanted badly to self-destruct.

However, they kissed my wounds and held my head up.

I kicked and I screamed, creating excuses in my head; but they hugged, and they whispered, giving answers instead.

The demons beckoned I leave and swim back in filthy ponds;

but they wouldn't let go, only holding on until the demons were gone.

They have forgiven me, where I've given up hope.

Believing in the best of me, when I could barely cope.

I am far from healed, but unconditionally they will remain all along.

Faithfully I am theirs and they are mine; we remain strong.

Chapter 1: Love

# Taurus & Pisces

The mighty Taurus went to the Brook to fetch itself a drink.

Before its lips touched water, Taurus fell in and began to sink.

Two fish named Pisces arrived and carried Taurus back to shore.

Taurus thanked Pisces and they replied; *"whatever for?"*

"You saved me," said Taurus, *"let me repay you for the act."*

*"We graciously decline,"* said Pisces, *"see you around old chap."*

Off Pisces went, into the deep blue, and Taurus watched them go until they were completely out of view.

Many a day's past before Taurus came back to water's edge, but Taurus wasn't alone, a bear was looking over the pier's ledge.

Taurus asked the bear, *"What are you doing?"*

The bear answered, *"catching rare fish, I'm waiting for them to start moving."*

Then the water began to ripple, and the bears claws reached in.

Taurus saw it was Pisces who was about to be eaten.

Taurus charged the bear, the two now in a fight.

The bear risking injury turned tail and took flight.

Pisces came to the surface, *"Thank you for saving our lives."*

"Don't mention it," said Taurus, *"I was just doing what's right."*

Against all odds, Taurus and Pisces became the best of friends.

Loving and looking after each other forever and beyond the end.

*Chapter 1: Love*

# Above My Own Depths

I will love your body as if it were my own.

But with greater admiration, because loving you without judgment is all I've ever known.

Because of you, I've had to redefine the definition of red.

Simply put, there's no color passionate enough to describe the seen or unsaid.

For my dear, you are more than woman...you are Godly.

# Be Not Afraid of Love

I am not afraid of love; I wear my heart on my sleeve.

In fact, I hold it in my hand because it's love I want you to believe.

Be not afraid of love.

Take off your armor, put down your masks.

Open thy arms to life, we should all smile and laugh.

Be not afraid of love.

For love is the base of creation.

We can share in its abundance; we can give, and love will grow.

Love should be what we all know.

Love is what bonds and love is what holds.

Love is what frees and what we can't let go.

## Chapter 1: Love

Be not afraid of love because love is unafraid of you.

Your heart can be desolate, but it's evil, love can undo.

Be not afraid of love, for it's in love with you.

Your heart may sing in blue, but it's love that can play the tune.

I am not afraid of love; I embrace it with all my might.

Shadows cower, run and hide when they are faced with love's light.

Be not afraid of love, it's not loving that hurts.

Love is real, love we can feel, love soothes pain because love can heal.

Be not afraid of love, wear your heart on your sleeve.

In fact, hold it in your hand and dare others to believe.

# When She Looks at Me

This is more of a story about the time I discovered Love.

Not the same type of love of friends and family.

Not traditional, unconditional, or the original.

This was deeper still.

Fathoms deeper than my heart could fathom.

An answer to a false truth staring me right in the face.

All my life, I thought I knew what love was and in one moment, in one look, that all changed.

Imagine me, painted glass, shattered, scattered and reassembled again.

It was a simple slice of time, brief, yet profound.

I held her in my arms, no different than any other day.

I looked upon her as she looked upon me and suddenly, in the embrace of her iris, I was bathed.

I was anything and everything, I was man and I was God, I was then, I was now and future to be. I was me, the best me I could ever hope to be.

It was all there, inscribed in the reflection of her eyes.

## Chapter 1: Love

A feeling, an emotion so vast it saw through my shell, wiped clean my sins of hell and spoke only to my realest self.

Understand, in one look she silenced all my cries for help.

It was unmistakable, only a fool could miss it and trust me, I've been that fool.

But not on this day, on this day she showed me something in LIFE, I've only felt nearing DEATH.

A presence so grand it could only be one thing...and now I know.

## My Final Wish

When I die...I hope it's while looking into your eyes.
Because the center of your iris is my gateway to heaven.

# IF OPRAH COULD HEAR MY WORDS

CHAPTER 2 OF 5

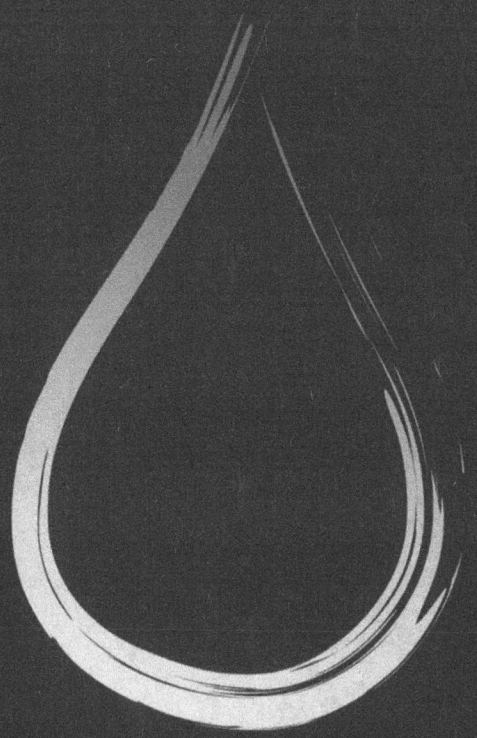

# HEARTBREAK

THIS CHAPTER IS ABOUT HEARTBREAK.

IT IS FULL OF TEARS AND CHRONIC PAINS.

LISTLESS AND DYING.

A SOUL WAS PEEN PIERCED.

WAITING TO BE MENDED.

LOVED AND RAISED UP.

IT IS ME.

## *Lacrimam*

If Oprah could hear my words, she would know I am a man written in heartbreak.

Written in the ways the weak prey upon innocence, or so easily give up soul mate for meaningless aspirations of grandeur.

If Oprah could hear my words, she would hear a heart that beats faintly under the subtle whispers of tears, quietly tiptoeing down an inward caving face.

Watch as my beauty fades, falling victim to sickness on the inside.

I am broken without will to mend and God will not forgive me of my sin.

If Oprah could hear my words, she would know I am a man written in heartbreak.

A subject to torture and a heart not worth a damn.

So, I close, keeping the love out and hiding myself from all of you.

If Oprah could hear my words, she would hear my cries amongst the cries of Cupid's lies. Bringing forth a brighter day, knowing it will end in a storm, leaving me with a gaping wound festering in torrential downpour.

How can I find happiness when all else pales in comparison to their touch?

If Oprah could hear my words, she would know we carry identical names, we are all pieces of illustrated poetry and we are all beautifully framed.

It is what ties us to everything, I believe it is our fate.

We are all heartbreak, we are the same, we are the human race.

*Chapter 2: Heartbreak*

# Simply Be Loved

All my life I have glanced at the sky, peering into the heavens imagining angels.

Splendid the thought, the one I'd rest with, snug in feathered wings of flight.

I Look deep into the moon's frozen path, making wishes on every star that falls in passing.

With every wish, my heart flutters in a dance of joy, but such dancing is short-lived, my own heart celebrates too soon, each wish failed coming true, until one star brought me to you.

I simply loved you and you simply loved me, you gave me a gift, which rivals all that could be.

Our love made me happy, it was honest and real, and the kiss sounded of harps, it was music I could feel.

I wish it could have lasted, the pain lingers like lashes from a belt and although it hurts, I am thankful for the love I found.

Relationships may end, but the kisses stain memories of a time when life was sweet and so here it is, the only wish I wish you'd keep.

Starlight, star bright, please grant me this wish tonight; to simply be loved.

*Chapter 2: Heartbreak*

# One + One =
## 1 + 1= 2.

But if 1 plus 1 equals 2, then the 1 next to me must be an improper fraction.

A seed covered under six feet of frozen snow, shadowed from the sun and receiving zero-foot candles.

Questioning, *"will it bloom?"* and equating to the answer of no.

Either that or I am standing in the wrong classroom, where the meaning multiply means to increase in quantity, but somehow 1 x 1 always equals one.

I'm trying to add up to an even number, but two does not exist to me.

# $1 + 1 = 2?$

More like 1 divided by the same equals 1.

A lonely problem for a number that should never be alone.

This 1 had a pair, we were 2 and then 2 wasn't there.

I was left counting, my numbers stanched between lips.

Stranded in the company of numbers who cannot exist without...you...without...two.

Life now a countless game, a painful game of hide and seek.

I count to 1, become stuck and never turn to peek because counting makes absolutely no sense to me.

## Chapter 2: Heartbreak

$$1 \times 1 = 1.$$

$$1 \div 1 = 1.$$

One plus one equals...well, it can't equal two until one and I unite because one and one equals 1 whole and that's what I'm solving for.

# No Hope

There's no hope for me, no hope at all.

I want, I wanted to find love so badly.

I did, I truly did, but even then, I was washed away by my tears, by my hurt.

There's no hope for a broken soul, no hope for a face beaten by relentless rain.

I hide my pain under waterways that work their way through my open heart, but there's no hope. No matter how many times I try, there's always no hope.

I tried waiting for love to come to me; no hope.

I tried searching as far and wide as I could see; no hope.

I tried and I tried, there's just no hope for me.

So, I leave you now with these last words.

Look at me and tell me, do you see what I see?

Hopelessness, there's no hope, no hope, not for me.

*Chapter 2: Heartbreak*

# Light of 1000 Angels

There is a light amid the mist of this foggy night.

A light who wanders aimlessly over the rocky waters, searches ocean's ripple until wave clashes wave and another light is found.

I watch the grandfather of time pass as its pendulum swings, counting my life down as more and more fireflies sing.

Lights streak the sky gleaming.

They're children of the sun joining the starry night, the heavens beautifully covered in freckles of light dancing about the milky way.

The sky glowing as the light of a thousand angels play.

I can hear them sing "*I love you*" into the gentle breeze.

This courtship a delight, I rise with loving might, but with broken wing such love is beyond my dimming light.

I reach my hand up for I am alone, the lights pass and rise as my heart further turns to stone.

I wish to join.

Braving fate I take a step forward, but down I go, falling deep into the rocky waters below.

The lights still brilliant, glowing in the sky, as I quiver and churn at the hurt, I'm feeling inside.

There's nothing I can do but bear witness to such a fairy tale fable.

The sole soul watcher from nowhere, as the light of a thousand angels play.

*Chapter 2: Heartbreak*

# *Cry Me a River*

Save your tears for another day.

Because love can be snuffed out quicker than the mafia rubs out a snitch.

Talking's cheap, similar to the feelings you said you had for me.

Go on…get!

The dog can run amuck, it's free, I've let go of the leash.

I'm not the kind; unlike yourself, to strangle and squeeze.

It's unfortunate though, the mechanics of you and I were geared to rule the world.

Yet dreams fade fast and you faded fast from me.

You fossilized quick and became ancient history.

You knew how I felt, how over the hills I went.

But I came back to the barn and it turns out you're not worth a cent.

It's a waste of time trying to help you see.

I stopped sweating the little stuff, that's why Ima let you be.

Life can be harsh, lessons learned hard to assist in moving up to higher ground.

The higher we climb, the more we can see one hundred and eighty degrees around.

I'm certain I'll see you in the future, when you've been kicked to the curb.

All I'll have to say to you is, cry me a river, and not another word.

*Chapter 2: Heartbreak*

# *I Lost You*

Once again, I build myself up only to fall.

Everything was great, the romance between us strong.

I wonder what happened, what did I do?

Where did the connection snap, was it me or was it you?

Lost in my feelings, did I throw them too fast?

Should I have given you space, is that why we didn't last?

Before I made a move, you were already gone.

One with mist you had already moved on.

Navy blue in color and deep like oceanic trenches.

The tears I shed are dark blue, adding depth to our distance.

I should never have said anything, what I felt inside was too strong.

I wish we could start over, maybe nothing would go wrong.

Arriving back at the beginning, I'd alter my depiction.

I can be what you want me to be, just give me the description.

I should have stifled my love until you were ready to hear.

Ready to invite me alongside, praising your love without fear.

But I pushed you into oblivion, I gambled with chance.

I rolled the dice and lost, I lost you in a passing glance.

*Chapter 2: Heartbreak*

# *Who?*

Who is it who said, "*I love you,*" but left?

Who is it who said, "*I'm with you,*" but turned their back?

You have me confused, because my heart is bruised.

I remember turning the knob and stepping through, then turning around and walking out the door.

I was present for a moment, then gone in a second.

In love for a lifetime but rejected at birth.

This love we created was aborted with no worth.

Words such reminisce now of happier times, parallel wallowing and painful memories that bind.

The devil who protected me is no different from the angel who killed me.

The guardian whom pierce deep into my back, leaving me lost, abandoned literally by light.

Left to pick up the scraps while blind and unable.

I believed your poetry, but this story was mere fable.

Who is it who said, "*I'll never leave*"?

Who is it who said, "*put all your trust in me*"?

I believe it was you, you left, and you lied.

Who now am I, a person that smiles and weeps?

Am I the one of heart, or the broken-hearted, and if I am not the one, then who?

## The Hand Dipped in Red

She was caught red-handed.

Abusing a romance, I thought together we banded.

Black lace and a surgical mask, she cuts open my sternum and proceeds to grasp.

She tugs and she pulls, squeezing a bleeding heart.

The pain is immense, the taste in my mouth is tart.

Beside me on the table are more instruments used to cut me.

I lay on this gurney wondering how could I be this unlucky?

Barehanded, she rips the ribs one by one from my cage.

Severs various arteries separating love from its grace.

I watch on as she yanks my life from my chest.

Leaving me strewn about in my own filth and my own flesh.

Her hands plunged into my soul, and I am now nothing because of everything she stole.

Cut down, such pain penetrated bones and gristle.

I am now traumatized by this tragedy; love is so brittle.

A promise now scarlet, she looks at me with those eyes no longer burning starlit.

She was caught red-handed, holding onto the heart she gouged out of me like an organ bandit.

Sharing my space with a stranger, someone else who now occupies my bed.

I am heartbroken and alone, I've been marked by the hand dipped in red.

*Chapter 2: Heartbreak*

# The Things I Did

I can't imagine the things I did.

At least, I can't believe I did what I did.

I viewed you as my queen and I wanted so badly to be the king.

However, your highness, I didn't come close.

I was a lowly servant at most.

Favor after favor, all tasks carried out.

I slaved and I slaved, worked and bled for you.

I thought I could please you, that my actions would make you fall for me.

All this time wasted, hoping for what would never be.

I look back now pained by the regret of you.

I gave you purest life of soul and you spit on a dying dog.

I gave thought of you, twenty-four hours and seven days a week.

I gave energy to what soon would be a meaningless and pointless dream.

I convinced myself to remain by your side through thick and thin.

But when the fat was cut you were the first to give up and give in.

You simply asked and it was done.

The majesty's will was my everything, it was my glowing sun.

Looking back with hindsight, I see a relationship quite glib.

I shake my head and laugh because I can't believe the things I did.

*Chapter 2: Heartbreak*

# *Puppet*

You opened me from my case, loved me and took care of me.

But in my dreams, you seemed to be carefully building a stage, building a stage around me.

I still loved you; my smile was carved perfectly from cheek to cheek.

You lightened my life; the spotlight above me was ever so radiant.

But in my dreams, such lights were shut off, I was performing in darkness, shrouded truth blurred by glass eyes only painted of false iris.

But still...I danced, I leaped, I moved, I did anything for you.

Then you started adding things to my arms, to my legs, things I think you called strings.

But still...I played, I laughed, I loved, I did anything for you.

However, I was just a toy to you, and I became your puppet.

Thrown about like a rag doll.

The only time I stood up was when you commanded, so you could see me fall.

You cut my strings, watched my listless body collapse and wooden heart break apart.

Here now I lay, helpless, trapped on a stage built by lies and all I can do is nothing.

You were the master and I, your puppet.

Chapter 2: Heartbreak

# Never Mine

I think back to the joyous times we had.

I think back to the times you made me so glad, to be me, the man I see.

I think back to the times when you were all that mattered.

You were mine and I yours, we were so in love.

I remember...I remember.

But it's painfully obvious now, you were never mine.

You were NEVER MINE to love, you were NEVER MINE to hold.

You were like the freezing cold.

You froze my hands till I could no longer feel, until I could no longer feel your warmth, no longer feel you, until I could not feel you at all.

You were never mine, never mine to begin with, you were never mine to end with.

You were like an echo, one I thought I heard, but hear no longer, you were an echo that faded, an echo that never happened at all.

For you were never mine.

You were NEVER MINE to kiss, NEVER MINE to make love to and feel a piece of sincere bliss, not in the heavens or on earth, not somewhere in between or on dirt, because you...you my dear...you were NEVER MINE, Never Mine, never mine at all.

*Chapter 2: Heartbreak*

# *Ripped*

As gentle and light as paper, I drifted from your hand and laid flat on the floor.

You never used me.

You never wrote on me.

You only crumpled me up and threw me far across the room.

I was stepped on, I was kicked, but you did the worst.

You ripped my edges and you ripped my seams.

You tore out all that made me whole.

I could have been a poem.

I could have been a plane.

I could have been your journal or simply had your name.

Possibilities were endless, I was your canvas, you the dreamer and I the dreamt.

But you did the unthinkable, you did the worst.

You ripped me up and threw me away.

# My Wasted Kiss

Before you, I never experienced a kiss.

My lips have always been solid and dry.

I was raised to think the first kiss meant the world.

So, I knew it had to be with one special girl.

When we kissed, I saw my world morph.

Where once stood a young boy now stood a young man.

My life flashed before my eyes and you were my wife.

So, it's sad to say, I wasted a kiss.

My first kiss, which was given to you.

A gift taken for granted.

I didn't want anyone else, but you walked away.

I honestly thought it'd take a miracle to find another woman come my way.

To find a kiss that seals the deal and two hearts connect as one.

I had that once, but as soon as it started, it was done.

I wasted my kiss, I treasured it and held it dear.

*Chapter 2: Heartbreak*

My kiss was used and abused, tossed out of an open window.

I trusted you because the kiss was a promise.

The kiss was a pact you broke and denied us.

I wasted my kiss and I can't get it back.

I gave it to you, and you threw it away, emptied it into the trash because my kiss was waste.

Yet, for life, my lips will be imprinted on yours, as your lips for life will be imprinted on mine.

Layers of kisses may arrive in time, but the first kiss will forever be there hidden underneath.

Therefore, my lips burn whenever I see you.

The acid you left heats immensely when you are near.

I'll never understand why something so good went so bad so quickly, but I do know I wasted my kiss and I wasted it on you.

# Book of Mine

This book of mine, filled with pages and words that create different stories with different meanings.

This book of mine, filled with pages of pain and some scorched with your fiery name.

This book of mine, filled with feelings, whatever I felt.

But you filled me with the most hurtful inspiration beyond any, without doubt.

Now I'm feeling hurt, sitting here, just sitting.

Staring at this my book of mine, not writing a word, just sitting here hurt.

Not even words can describe how agonizing this wound is.

My open flesh festers and I struggle to speak words wealthy enough in emotion to convey crippled limbs of lively tumultuous torture.

This book of mine, filled with pages and words written of misery from a time I find loathing. This book of mine, filled with pages forged from the darkest depths of my ego.

## Chapter 2: Heartbreak

Dripping in hate, screaming of truth, that you should know because you caused it.

Every bitter, sour, unsweetened morsel that I was forced fed.

This book of mine, filled with pages as a dedication to our love.

It reads: Farewell, our love is too far gone.

This book of mine unfinished, true love undone.

This is my final passage; our love is done.

# By the River

By the river, I'm waiting for you.

By the river, I say to myself, I love you.

By the river, I see your face gently floating in the river so blue.

People that pass tell me, *"get over it, you're through, find someone else more suitable for you."*

But I can't, I won't, because I'm still in love with you.

I feel one day we'll meet again.

By the river, I wait now, and I'll wait then.

By the river, silence echoes through.

All I hear is the laughter of you.

By the river, I sit and wait.

By the river, I see a butterfly and its beauty reminds me of you, color burst of radiant flush flutters away with breeze.

Come back soon, I want to hold you again, but until then my heart must wait.

By the river, I'm writing these words to you.

## Chapter 2: Heartbreak

**By the river, I say to myself, "this poem is for you."**

**By the river, I'll keep waiting for you.**

# Does Love Last Forever?

Answer me this or answer me not, how long do I have before my heart stops?

Before the vibrant glow of new fades and I become dark, desolate and dismal with shade?

When will the parade die?

Where in time do smiles tell lies, while lovers stare deeply into the other's eyes and find they do not appreciate their prize?

Could it be it's all an illusion, meant to deceive and trick the deluded?

Meant to prank poor souls into thinking their hearts have concluded?

Thus, banishing them into loneliness where they can only feel excluded?

I once believed in such magic, until truth revealed its deception and I falling stagnant.

I would wait in the building until detonation by the foreman because time and time again this tragedy was my torment.

*Chapter 2: Heartbreak*

Then, down it would all go, level-by-level, gravel and dust falling like snow.

A captain drowning with his ship, fainting under darkness thinking; will I miss it?

Maybe I'm just a child who is easily bored.

Some are fine with one, but I desire the sorts.

It is true I am young, lost and obviously not that clever.

Maybe I will never find my answer to; does love last forever?

# Haunted Heart

I have a haunted heart.

The love I had drifted away from me like a ghost vanishing through walls.

However, their spirit remains.

Visions created by my love walk in my heart for all days and more.

When I close my eyes, I see nothing, but a broken heart and you shattered in the distance.

When I try to grasp you, hold you, in the warmth of soft embrace, demons throw me from where I stood, back to a cage restraining me from you.

The more I struggle and attempt to break free, the darker my visions get, the harder it is to see.

Soon I won't have you in my dreams.

I will forget the memory.

But you will always be seen in my heart and without any apathy.

## Chapter 2: Heartbreak

**Because my soul, my heart, is haunted with your love and through blackest night and darkest day, you'll be the lost love that never faded away.**

# *Fire*

My passion for you is like the fire that burns at the end of a candle.

As the fire burns, the wick blackens and curls, but the fire gets thicker and burns much brighter.

That's how much I love you.

Heat from the fire melts down the wax, which streams down the side; that's my warming tears, slowly trickling from my hazel eyes.

Oh, how I miss you.

Heat from the fire is so intense, so hot, your hand burns when placed over the flame.

The same happens when my hand is placed over my bosom, where my heart beats in your name.

I realized now as long as the fire burns within, my love for you will never die.

What I feel is a forever flame, ever consuming, always raging with searing touch.

Until I find you, my fire will keep on burning.

## Chapter 2: Heartbreak

The wax will keep on dripping and my love for you will keep on growing because you are my fire, you keep me going.

# *I Thought I'd Found You*

I came to this place because I thought I would find you.

Like in a romantic comedy, I believed we'd meet perhaps due to some strange cosmic coincidence.

We'd find the irony and, against all odds by the climax, it would be just us.

I looked for years.

Never did I see you; never did I hear a peep of a pin drop.

It was empty, just like the others, silent and still, I was the only life to inhabit the room.

I came to this place to be by your side, kneel upon one knee, and confess my undying love for thee.

Hold you in compassionate arms of novel's embrace and kiss you...finally kiss you!

I traveled far, and I traveled wide, hoping that somehow, we'd collide in this ever-twirling tornado of love.

I came to this place, the place where we began, slaying unworthy suitors dreaming the search would end.

*Chapter 2: Heartbreak*

Odysseus reuniting with Penelope, but breath beheld I must amend.

I find instead, my search continues.

I was fooled by this farse, romance and fairy tales.

Tricks played on emotional cards held in heart's hand.

I thought I would find you here, but I was wrong.

# Unforgettable

At one point you were here, but as time raced with speed, you vanished without a trace and I without ability to track.
I often wonder what happened, I wonder where you went.

It's been so long since our presence dwelled together.

Is it petty that I miss you as much as I tend to?

Your voice still echoes softly amidst invisible air, as if you are here next to me whispering in my ear.

Everything about you loops like a record, the song of you repeating, sticking in my head because you're infectious.

Our hearts did not entwine, although I wish different.

It burns knowing we were friends, but I dreamed of so much more.

Beautiful you were in secret; beautiful you were to me.

I wish I could have said what it is I am truly feeling, however you disappeared before this magician's final revealing.

## Chapter 2: Heartbreak

I've pulled the cover and I don't know where you've gone to.

Alone on stage, I stand in illusion, basking in unforgettable you.

I couldn't confess my love then, so I spoke of it to the moon.

I said at least this to the ghost of you; did you know that you are unforgettable?

# What It Means to See

Film images flicker before me.

I watch moments come, and I watch moments go.

In, and out, they appear, and fade.

A puzzle viewed by eyes and pieced together by head.

Images reversed in time like words flipped when read.

The colors I see, developed somewhere in the infinite with my sense of me, processed, and printed somewhere in the outer limits.

I believe I know what is real.

Able to sense the difference between a moment in a scene, and my movie reel.

I think, therefore I am, and therefore I...

...I feel my flesh burning from the distance of your touch.

I taste my mouth souring from the missing of your lips.

I smell nothing from the absences of your scent.

I hear mummers from the silence of your sound, and I see the life I thought we had, but never was.

## Chapter 2: Heartbreak

A film unwinding and unspun.

A cinematic rewound and undone.

So, what does it mean to see?

It means to see the movie you thought you were filming, but never filmed at all.

A reverse image, envisioned, but lost.

# Broken Love

Sandwiched between two mirrors, I reflect infinitely.

My pulsing heart sending ripples across glass, and the glass rippling back a reflection of my infinitely expanding love.

I know its power; I feel its warmth.

It is soothing, ever embracing, and yet I stand alone.

Reflecting to myself, by myself, in a circling cycle, celebrating countless crying cold nights of loneliness.

Hear me, mirror, mirror on the wall, tell me one of these reflections show her in my embrace no matter how small.

Two eyes locked with mine.

Gentle arms wrapped around my chest with tender kiss.

Two drums beating between the reflection of endless love.

Tell me mirror, tell me she's there, somewhere in the infinite spectrum of your reflection.

Somewhere passed this face with sorrowful frown, a face that reflects a cadaver who's drowned.

*Chapter 2: Heartbreak*

A man who cannot breathe because he is many depths into his pain.

A man who cannot heal because he is many cuts into his veins.

I tremble in the presence of your silence, as I fear truth.

Forgive me as I break you.

Shattering a hope that will never be.

Leaving me alone, with seven years bad luck, between two mirrors and my broken love.

# Stupid Cupid

I hate you...stupid cupid, God of desire, I hate you!

I curse Eros, he fathered a mean son.
The God of love created not a cherub, but a demon.
It punctured my innocent heart, guilty only of being without love, and then twisted the inertial arrow until I gave up.

Once was enough, but it encouraged me to go again.

It made promise after promise until I finally gave in.

The worst decision I could have made, why did I listen?

Cupid is an imposter and pain is its mission.

Need proof?

Then please pull this deceitful blade from my back, hand it to me, bloody as is, so I can give it right back.

I'll stab cupid deep and gouge out its heart.

I'll show cupid agony, and what it feels like to be torn apart.

I curse Eros, he fathered a mean son.

## Chapter 2: Heartbreak

The God of love created not a cherub, but a demon.

The Devil is a lie, and cupid tricked me into thinking I could be loved.

But still I fell...fell head over heels and onto my knees, bleeding out in a field of roses absent of birds and bees.

Cupid, you're no angel, just the Devil in disguise, and I swear, one day cupid, it'll be your turn to die.

# Never Cry Again

It was a warm night and my slumber was sweet.

Her arms snug around me like a blanket with heat.

Here, I felt safe, as though I could live forever.

No monsters, devils, or beasts could harm me here, ever.

However, on this night I pressed my ear against her bosom; something was wrong, her breathing had frozen.

Nightmares breached mind, striking fear in love's holding.

My only fear, that by time I woke, I would no longer be her chosen.

Just a husk of my former self, a scarecrow emptied out and left open.

Miles stretched between us; something wasn't right.

We shared the same bed, but she was out of my sight.

Feelings felt deep, became too cold to touch and before I could sayith one word, my skin had already been slashed and cut.

*Chapter 2: Heartbreak*

Like nails to a chalkboard, my ears cringed as she spoke in tongues.

Each line swarmed of bees, and I stood there, allowing myself to be stung.

With broken heart in hand, I stood amongst a dying field of roses.

Tears flooded from forested eyes while the green burned beneath the surface.

The embrace was long, but I could only sense her leaving.

I am away from the moment; I had already begun grieving.

She straddled a pale horse and I waved goodbye to death.

I don't think she knows this, but her fatal absence was almost my last breath.

My tears ran dry that day, a valley of death that won't amend.

Because of that hardship, I will never cry for her, or any woman ever again.

# A Man Made of Ice

When the world was young, man was full of life.

But all it takes is one heartbreak, to make a man made of ice.

By nature, we want to love, but the world can be cruel.

Tempted by darkness, many a man can be fooled.

We are hard-shelled brutes in search of gentle embrace.

Life can be bitter, but love is the sugar sweet we long to taste.

Man was bred from dirt, and woman from apart of him.

The protector of a fragile heart, she is the missing rib.

Man's Achilles heel, a permanent hole in our chest.

Man may appear to be impervious, but a woman can penetrate his breast.

And if she so chooses, to cripple the man before thee, the widows bite will decompose his honor from king to unworthy.

The man that once was, will become nothing more than mulch.

## Chapter 2: Heartbreak

He will seep into the dirt and further into the blood gulch.

His old image petrified, a tombstone in memoriam of his former self.

A beast now rises from dry ice, who consumes the hearts of beauties and nothing else.

His warmth has long faded, all that remains is cold.

The only thing to save him is the right love to hold.

When the world was young, man was full of life.

But all it takes is one heartbreak to make a man made of ice.

# Beneath These Golden Lights

There is no other instant we exist in.

Behind this closed door there is only our existence.

I am promised only a moment, but you graciously give me forever and I selfishly say forever is never enough, but with you, how could it be...ever?

Beneath these golden lights, I am lost in the soft glow of your touch, rendered helpless by the allure of your scent and trapped by the branches of your wilderness.

A forest glazed beneath these golden lights.

Sweeter than honey, worth more than money.

I am in the presence of someone divine.

A deity of sorts, possibly Aphrodite in the flesh.

Dare I say I've been hit with an arrow in the chest?

An arrow dipped in the very thing I fear I am forbidden to bare from my breast.

Because we do not exist in any other instant except beneath these golden lights and I am a fool for being tempted into that pool, but your depth is the kind that I like.

## Chapter 2: Heartbreak

What a predicament, right?

You, the apple in the tree in a paradise made for me.

Ripe and full of flavor; your fruit looks to me beckoning.

Do I go against the word of God and pull from the one tree I was told I shouldn't?

Do I speak into our existence the one word I said I wouldn't?

Beneath these golden lights, you are the most beautiful anything to behold and everything within me wants to worship you from head to toe.

You are my escape, my drug, my excellence.

Therefore, I curse time whenever it brings upon our exodus.

If I could bend this reality, I'd gladly remain in the hold of your gravity.

But as soon as you appear beneath these golden lights, you are gone again, lost to the starry night and I am left with only a memory of our existence.

The only instant we exist in.

Behind closed doors and beneath these golden lights.

# Mistress

To my mistress, my muse, the sultry music in my room.

I am in awe of thee, before me is a portrait that I am unworthy of, a sculpture that has been sculpted from pure ivory tusks.

A vessel so beautiful, I idol much, and with the time I have, it's not enough.

So, I hold fast to dreams, day and night, night and day, and time still escapes me, even there you must go away.

Oh, how I hate to wake from our play!

A dance I wish would continue beyond the ballroom floor.

A song I wish could be sung outside the concert halls.

Life can be so unfair but if it wasn't for this; maybe I wouldn't have seen you anywhere?

Maybe our lives would have never intertwined, and I wouldn't care.

Maybe this is the only path we could ever share?

## Chapter 2: Heartbreak

Either way, there are rules to this, and to break them I would never dare but I swear, behind your stare there's something there.

A light, a glow, something far deeper than we can ever go.

It is to that light I am attracted like a moth, a line in the sand I feign to tread across.

To my mistress, my muse, the only color in my room.

I just want you to know...how can I say?

In another lifetime, I hope we can meet the right way.

# Trust Me

Trust, arguably the most important agreement between two people.

It levels the playing field, making the other and you equal.

Trust is a blind bond that delves deeper than the soul.

It is a promise we make to God because it takes a leap of faith to jump down that rabbit hole.

Only the divine knows where such promises lead.

One must be strong to trust, not weak.

Look at how far we've come, imagine where we'll be in the next hundred.

Nothing we see before us could have been accomplished unless someone was trusted.

Good or bad, we place our trust in the circle of life.

Everything happens for a reason...at least that's what we tell ourselves, right?

I trust you, and you trust me, it's the only way we can sustain humanity.

## Chapter 2: Heartbreak

I know it didn't seem like it, but I trusted you were the one and you poured into this bottomless pit hoping I would overflow with light like sun.

However, I am no celestial star, I'm just another man with a gun.

Another young minded, foul-mouthed, dick-swinging dude trying to have fun.

I trusted you, and you trusted me.

We made promises that I broke, and now judgment is upon me.

You can call me a backstabber, or a beast with two faces.

Either way, I took advantage of your faith, and shall be found guilty in all cases.

I say again, trust is a must; the most important agreement between two people and until I can truly understand that, I will never be your equal.

...Trust me.

# I Am Not a Monster

Do not judge me for my thoughts, temptation anchors inside primitive flesh.

Carnal desires, the valley of Sodom and Gomorrah, here I am her prisoner, a slave to Aphrodite.

Fantasies abloom, I dream of many women.

Greed and thirst for beauties consume my positive intuitions.

Be they drug, or be they addiction? I cannot stop wanting more, I cannot shake this hunger.

These eyes worship sex and feminine design with wonder.

Your image, her image, their image, my mind must collect.

Lips hindered helpless in the squeeze of her corset.

While making love with my partner, my mind has sex with an illusion.

What is wrong with me, why do I fuck this confusion.

I am not a monster; I just can't help this feeling!

*Chapter 2: Heartbreak*

This doesn't mean I love you any less, I'm just lost in the meaning.

Satisfaction at the push of a button.

Pressure released and our moment relinquished into nothing.

I wonder silently to myself; what is my idea of love coming to?

I know this is wrong but what else am I supposed to do?

The world my candy store, stocked with many assortments.

As I, the man, physically resists, although inner reptiles wish to adorn them.

I reminisce past fornications like pornographic reels on replay.

Reliving lost scenes of pleasure subjected to the same sick decay.

Dare I say, I am not a monster; but nor am I a man.

I'm more of a beast in need, sinking deeper into quicksand.

I beg of thee, forgive my obsession for plums, cherries, and peaches.

Drowning in a vat of filth, I succumbed to my weakness.

I know there is no excuse, I say this without attempt to justify, but I am not a monster, just a man who can't be satisfied.

*Chapter 2: Heartbreak*

# I Deserve

This I did what I did, so hate me.

Judge me, abuse me, do whatever you want, so long as you hate me.

Hit me, scream at me, I want to feel your fire, burn my flesh till charred.

Leave me searing in the wake of your anger, hate me.

Beat me, scratch me, cut me, make me bleed over your blade.

Force it in, twist till I shout, and then choke me until my words become gasps.

Stitch barbs through my lips like claps.

Keep me from speaking, tell me how much you hate me.

Call me the Devil, address me by my true name.

Hurt me until my tears run red.

Torture me until all has been said.

Inflict the worst of you, and then put it onto me.

Punish me my love, end me!

I am dirty and immoral.

I am a pig and I am nothing.

What have I done? You deserved none of this.

So, kill me if you must.

Hate me.

Chapter 2: Heartbreak

# Giving up on Love

I'm giving up on love, let love burn.

Love is stupid, love is pointless, I'm giving up on love because it gave up on me.

Cupids golden arrows soar, but the one meant for me has a poisonous tip.

I couldn't even be brought back with tender kiss.

Not after being struck in tender hip.

Therefore, I'm giving up on love.

It's let me down one too many times.

I don't see the point in going any further.

Love hasn't lifted my spirit or shown me fervor, but I have felt it break.

It's done nothing for me except cause more heartache.

I have no light, and I have no life.

I have run this race, and I am tired.

I am giving up on love and I won't return.

Love has given up on me, so, let love burn.

# Fish of Plenty

I am the fisherman and I am the fish.

I am alone and I am home.

I am lost and I am found.

I searched land, and water, but I am up as I am down.

I sail the seven seas; are they looking for me?

I cast my line; I think it's mine.

I feel a tug; I dream of hugs.

I will not miss; I dream of gentle kiss.

I cannot endure heartbreak; I hope I am the one their heart takes.

I reel them in; I'm hoisted from the water.

I gaze upon my catch; I see a sailor with an eyepatch.

I don't like what I see; I accept you despite who you may be.

I throw them back into the ocean and somehow, we are both broken.

Oh well, I guess there are plenty of fish in the sea.

Chapter 2: Heartbreak

# *When We Fight*

Release me from this, I wish not to engage.

Raising my weapon against you means it is to myself I take aim.

The iron is red.

To douse with water, they'll vaporize, or to place further into the fire and we'll burn.

I cannot be too close, but neither can I run.

The ocean settles on its own and I merely ride the waves.

My heart torn in two, cut apart by razor blades.

It's hard to speak out of fear of drawing them upon me.

No love be perfect, no love be lovely.

How I wish this could be avoided.

Each protest rotting the best part of me.

I am not comfortable with such unfamiliarity.

Conceit; I must conceit.

Pride will be our defeat; alas I conceit.

Sadly, giving way will not save us.

It will not change what must.

But standing against you is aching, I wither and become dust.

I hate the fighting, why are we at odds?

Perhaps we must journey through this valley together.

Confront galling winds, side by side, birds of a feather.

Please do not reject my hand, for we are our only guides and the only thing I hope is, happily ever after awaits us on the other side.

*Chapter 2: Heartbreak*

# A Bee Without Nectar

The bee whom cannot indulge in the flower, or the spider whom cannot have the prey in its web.

What you want most, held just out of reach.

Love so close, but still a fantasy.

Abstract and unusual, both painful and pleasurable.

I am hurting when they are near, and I am hurting when they are not.

Happiest when they are here and regretting the time we never got.

Best friends and lover's sweet, romantic twine whenever our eyes meet.

Pulled apart but forever reaching towards one another.

What cruel fate to have never been discovered what could have been?

What blossoms would we see, how far into the stars would we be?

Soul mates in waiting, perhaps soul mates from another place.

Unknowingly tracing a familiar path back to lover's lake.

The flower whom cannot give itself to the bee, or the fly whom the spider cannot have its way with.

I am in love, but that love remains just out of reach.

A bridge uncrossed because of a promise I must keep.

To sully newest love, in turn, spoils what beckons.

So, unless fated to be, I must live with my obsession.

Right there in front of me.

Ever so close...yet, still so far away.

*Chapter 2: Heartbreak*

# *The Cheated Turned Cheater*

Dealing of the prior, hurt held deep will often creep.

Find its way through catacombs because closeted skeletons are hard to keep.

I was innocent, my only crime loving more than I could know.

An eager beaver testing how large his damn could grow.

No, I was a vibrant red meadow soon to be killed by snow.

Blanketed in coldest ice.

My betrothed would submit to cruelest vice.

Testing limitations of my morality, not once...but twice.

My heart and soul was taken by a thief in the night.

Leaving behind a broken shell amongst a sea of beached fossils, I am bleached and white.

Swearing I'd never cause the same pain which conjures thoughts of ending life.

I spoke too soon. Like day into night, I would become the moon.

I underestimated unresolved issues and married with depression; my troubles would bloom.

I was a vibrant red meadow, my betrothed loved me so.

Picking at my flowers, there was nowhere they wouldn't go.

But my pollen was poisonous, neither of us knew.

A body lay in my field now, a regret I cannot undo.

Sins of another became sins of my own.

My love distorted and misshapen, I am alone.

I have been bitten; the monster is me.

Forgive me not, I am unworthy of mercy.

*Chapter 2: Heartbreak*

# Losing My First Love

*"This just in, the world as we know it is coming to an end.*
*We have reports that an extinction level event is inevitable.*
*It is on course to strike our home without warning.*
*This is not a test, I repeat, this is not a test."*

Nothing can prepare you for Armageddon.
Not when you're in love, not when you can't come down from this wonderful feeling.
I broke through my ceiling, I thought this would last forever.
However, watching their mouth move was like watching the worst news ever.

*"To avoid mass panic and prolonged chaos.*
*The government decided to keep this object a secret.*
*They believed they could change its course but failed.*
*We urge citizens to take this time to make their final preparations."*

Everything appeared to be picture perfect, I had house with a gate, and green grass.
"It's too good to be true" I'd say to myself, but still, I believed it last.
God damn, just when I thought I'd heard it all.
I go to turn off the TV, but wait, there's an emergency call.

*"Ladies and gentlemen, it's over, contact has been made.*
*It'll only be moments before we are all taken out by the shockwave.*
*If you're watching this now, thank you for tuning in.*
*Unfortunately, there won't be a next time, signing off, farewell my friends."*

Everything goes silent, then the ground starts to quake.
My legs buckle under their own weight as the entire world shakes.
A glow rises over the horizon, a tidal wave of fire and light.
Then...there's nothing, nothing sadly ever after.
At least, that's what it feels like right?

Chapter 2: Heartbreak

# *Beautifully Blinded*

I was a fool.

An idiot, stupid, dumb and naive.

How could I have allowed myself to believe, someone like you could ever love someone like me.

She's beautiful and he's bad.

She's sexy and he's smoking hot.

They fine as hell, he a fuck boy and she's a thot.

Ten out of ten, if looks could kill?

Echo and Narcissus are real.

Facades of Greek gods and goddesses, bodies of the divine define sublime palaces.

Demi-Gods, Angels on Earth.

These babies had them good, good genes since birth.

It was love at first sight, the second I laid eyes upon them.

But I also lost sight of self, the second they laid eyes upon me.

I was a fly willingly throwing itself into a spider's web.

Anxious to be caught, cocooned, and devoured.

They could do no wrong, I worshipped the ground they walked along.

They were my sky, a breath of fresh air.

I didn't live for myself only for their needs and care.

Giving all I had, all of my precious gifts.

Fangs sunk deep, the numbing of leeching lips.

I gave, and they took.

I wanted them to love me, I made them my dream.

But they were no one of substance, they were hollower than me.

It's hard to comprehend that beauty can act as a blindfold.

When all I had was a hand full of fool's gold and still, I claimed I was rich.

My eyes are now open to the truth.

But unfortunately, it took getting hurt and used.

I learned my lesson; beauty doesn't mean shit.

## Chapter 2: Heartbreak

I swear I'll never mistake diamonds for white sapphires again.

Lies are thin like cards and like cards they can be used for illusion.

To deceive and make believe this trick is magic.

The hands alone are not always quicker than the eye.

Many times, the eyes tell the tale but it's the mouthpiece that always sells the sale.

# Distrust

I was raped.

No, I said no!

Still, it came.

The seed, small.

Over time, undeniable.

This is our baby.

A result of two.

Not the child we wanted.

A face full of scorn.

I hate the baby.

I wish it could be aborted.

But it can't.

So, here we are.

Raising a child.

A wedge between us both.

A fetus that becomes disgust.

Chapter 2: Heartbreak

# *Disgust*

Distrust festers into nausea.

I want to vomit.

Your touch repulsive.

I squeeze our child.

A reminder of the rape.

It haunts me, as I am filled.

My insides bursting.

Your scent causes cramps.

I want you to vanish.

How I do not care.

But I know your presence.

It is reason I look to death.

To leave you alone with our baby.

Our child born from your sin.

I can't love you anymore.

I won't forgive.

# Deserted in an Insta

This monogamy was a pretty picture.

Photographed and Insta filtered.

A perfect, polished portrait perhaps posted in poor taste.

Remember when a picture was worth more than a thousand words?

Today, pictures tell more than a thousand lies.

Pissing in the pupils of people, presenting a performance, practical, and believable.

Even I, through mine eyes, thought we'd go the distance.

If this be the only evidence, you'd swear we'd last longer than an instant.

And here I thought dreams came true.

They do but don't be fooled by airbrush and distorted truth.

One image captured what I hoped would be the rest of my life, it turned out to be a false reality and a waste of my time.

*Chapter 2: Heartbreak*

Left with only questions and the misery of not knowing why.

The still speaks of two love birds but in fact, I didn't even get a goodbye.

# Holding on to Nothing

I wish I could hate you.

I can't.

I wish I could kill you.

I can't.

Maybe you could hate me.

You won't.

Maybe you could kill me.

You won't.

Remember when you left?

That hurt.

Remember when you moved on.

That hurt too.

You don't love me anymore.

I know.

You haven't in a very long time.

I know.

*Chapter 2: Heartbreak*

There's a void in your heart.

I feel it.

An emptiness where I used to be.

I feel it.

You've discarded everything we were.

I see it.

Charred and burning in the trash.

I see it.

But still, I hold on to something.

I have it.

I hold on to you.

I want it.

I am holding on to nothing.

So be it.

# Songbird

You should have left me in the wild before catching me in your net.

Taking me into your home, clipping my wings and forcing me to sing...forcing me to sing your song.

From this cage, I am flightless and flutter about.

I'm claustrophobic, and I am without breath.

I am feathers fluffed of stress and the song you believe is beautiful, is in fact, my daily plea for death to come, for death to end my song.

Because all I sing is sorrow, as I am placed by a window.

Ignored until it so pleases you and kept full with empty seeds.

It is from this prison I envy the sky.

Singing a sad song of a time before.

A time I will never see for I see you have grown tired of me, tired of my song.

From the air, I was taken to be thrown to the ground.

With one stomp, I am now splattered red.

## Chapter 2: Heartbreak

> Flightless, starved and caged.
>
> It never really mattered.
>
> I was already dead.

# The Timid Turtle

Inside of a shell lived a turtle.

A tiny turtle too timid to move.

The world abroad was too big and the turtle too afraid to lose.

One day another turtle appears, slowly crossing a rocky path.

Courage pumps into the timid heart and our turtle makes a move at last.

Over rock and rubble, they climb, suffering scrapes and many bruises.

Moving at a faster pace, hoping to catch up in time.

The timid turtle approaches, baring bravest soul.

The other, not amused, rejecting their proclaimed devotion.

Once upon a time, there was a turtle whom believed they were worthy of love.

Now they remain tucked in their shell, too timid and too hurt to believe they could ever be the one.

*Chapter 2: Heartbreak*

# *Lotus Flower*

The hardest part of loving is the unveiling of the inner me.

Sacred and fragile, it is more naked than my body.

To be the lotus, for them, you must blossom.

Bare your flower and be beautiful.

Exposed, open, and vulnerable.

This is the hardest part.

Why I fear being the lotus.

To open and not truly be noticed.

To give but not be in your focus but only a smudge of your vision.

A wilting floral, unsupported upon water.

So, I break and fall beneath, and it is here I would drown.

I am afraid to love.

Because all that would be left of me is a petal floating atop the ponds edge.

It is there in the shadows I would remain...unnoticed.

# IF OPRAH COULD HEAR MY WORDS

CHAPTER 3 OF 5

# ANGUISH

THIS CHAPTER IS ABOUT ANGUISH.

IT IS APATHY AND FIRE.

SCREAMS FROM THE DARKEST ROOM.

A SOUL BOUND BY DEATH.

WAITING TO BE NOTHING.

BLEEDING AND UNFINISHED.

IT IS ME.

# Flamma

If Oprah could hear my words, she would know I am a man written in anguish.

Written in the way's adversity scripts scars of stories, or how the sheer weight of misfortune turns tragedy into melancholy.

If Oprah could hear my words, she would hear a voice looking to share tales of plight along a journey.

Travelers beware, at the top of this mountain there is only death but yield not to this warning…carry on.

If Oprah could hear my words, she would know I am a man written in anguish.

A poem meant to open the literary minds of those dejected and bring forth truth silenced; we are of God's light and therefore tested.

If Oprah could hear my words, she would hear my sonnet amongst the tortured screams of vigil. Soothing the sorrow of nightfall for disparity can be blissful.

Bodies resist the pain and ailment woven into the fabric that covers the wound.

Strife is as much a part of life as life itself begins in the womb.

If Oprah could hear my words, she would know we carry identical names, we are all pieces of illustrated poetry and we are all beautifully framed.

It is what ties us to everything, I believe it is our fate.

We are all anguish, we are the same, we are the human race.

Chapter 3: Anguish

# The Anguish of Living

Surviving means being willing to die.

Dying so that one can be born over and over and over again.

Such torture for freedom, it is anguish but it is life.

Our cycle until we cycle no more.

A fissure between cracks whose pain knows no bounds.

A fact between two palms who gives not a single ounce.

# An Angry Man

An angry man, there is my story.

Written in a book swallowed by shadows, scorched by fire, frozen in ice, and slowly corroded with time in a chaotic heart.

'Twas once paradise here but now corrupted.

Apathy, hate and revenge, chemicals in lust for unbalance between Heaven and Hell, Olympus and Hades, where I alone feel ail, while they stand to mock me from my cell.

I see thy windows of opportunity growing darker by the second, but larger by the day.

Foul taunting whilst I am locked away.

Silenced by screams, decayer of dreams, shackled and robbed of my glory.

Therefore, an angry man, there is my story.

Summarized in three words, spewing out blood that breathe into me a life tainted by evil. Dangling emotion overhead, placing burden upon mortal soul by quarreling tooth between titans.

## Chapter 3: Anguish

I long to see death handed out by these hands, for I am a man fueled with anger.

Igniting what will be my legacy, I wince to think of how I became this.

Dare I say; I place blame upon Gods.

For I know not the answers to the universe but of this I am certain; wherever there is light, darkness is sure to follow.

So, when they speak my name as you have, when they ask of stories and poems as you have, let it be known when they ask of me; an angry man, there is his story and nothing more.

*~Inspired by*

*Homer's "The Iliad"*

# Words Worth

I was a poet and the teller of stories glee, writing sonnets like Shakespeare plenty.

People from all around would splendor, my words were said to carry great vigor.

Yet this was a time before I vanished, a time long before I was damaged.

This was a time when words held worth, before the pain, the hurt and the worst.

She was my everything, inspiration for illustrating happiness.

It was her absolute absence that caused me to regress backwards.

I remember it snowing, how white the room.

Anger filled my eyes; despair began to bloom.

Book by book I went, ripping out their contents.

I was a blind man, I never thought to look.

Candlelight lit the room, and the snow went ablaze.

I was caught in the inferno of my own rage.

## Chapter 3: Anguish

Love turned to hate, and I tore my heart to shreds.

As the ashes trickled down, I suddenly knew I was dead.

In the dark woods I live, writing the stories of the lost.

I give life to the faceless ones like me; here and the gone.

I search for every page, in hopes to repair my life.

To mend and bind my books of words worth, once upon a time.

# *Into the Dark Woods*

I have a story to tell, a story about a place where ghosts dwell.

Our shadows outlined in ink because it is where souls fell.

A lake of despair boiling with tar.

Swallowing the lives of many with their bleeding scars.

Children of the dark woods, share with me your blood.

Allow my crows to peck and taste the pain beneath the mud.

The silence of screams, your stories can live.

I will write them, and to them new life I will give.

The dark woods speak.

Ghosts of shadows past rise from creek.

We are the bodies who must face the forbidden serpent or fight the beastly bear.

The faithless who lie to themselves about their existence in nowhere.

Coyotes under moonlight, howling for lost souls.

Hoping our lovers find us while into the fray we go.

Voices muted, clocks broken into thirds.

Father time hath edged us at the end of our own words.

So, who am I but the faceless man who writes of these stories.

Pages I will share because they are my final glory.

I died long ago, a poet under ashes mourning.
He who writ himself into forlorning.

From fire and brimstone, mine book, singed and cooked with mine flesh.

Woven and sewn together reeking of putrid breath.

Children, my children, welcome to the dark woods, where your fears are kept.

A place in the middle of nowhere, where the sun fire burns until nothing is left.

# How Is It to Die?

Slipping into eternal darkness?

Where chaos is peace and pain is pleasure.

Where a heart which speaks aloud, speaks no longer.

What is it like once time becomes irrelevant?

Do trees still sway?

Do clouds plume with bird's melody, illuminating portraits of life just before your last breath?

**Tell me, how is it to die?**

When crows flock, do shadows form?

When tears dry, and pupils open as the door we cross is unveiled, do apparitions come?

After all this time I'm anxious to know, what is behind that open door?

**I wonder, how is it to die?**

When blood pools below a lifeless body, or air is pressed from expanding lungs, when silence is actually noisy, and feeling is more absent than numb...what is it like?

How does it feel?

## Chapter 3: Anguish

**Tell me, how is it to die?**

When the murder gathers, and death stands near?

What bright image is your last before fading into that warm blanket?

When scent fades from memory, what final thought does it take with it?

Before you go, I must know!

Fire so hot, air so cold, do not leave me in this world alone.

But here I am.

Staring deep into their eyes, lost.

Emptiness I can feel, a sorrow I can taste; I'm engulfed by black flames with this question echoed in my mind.

**I wonder, how is it to die?**

I beg of you; answer me!

I'm crying in my grave for I should have been disposed of.

How unfair, my life kept whole and yours thrown to the wind.

I wonder now unlike then, what it is like to cross that fatal line?

I've been spared and I need to know.

When time becomes irrelevant, do trees still sway?

Do clouds begin to fall?

Do crows mourn your passing as this life disappears?

Stay with me, slip not into that long-awaited slumber.

Whisper with final breath, shed sight on the blind I walk amongst in the night.

**Tell me, how is it to die?**

Their reply, "*dark.*"

*Chapter 3: Anguish*

# Death

So, what is death?

Death is what you fear.

Death is cold, death is heartless, death is blind, and death is deaf.

Death is non-emotion, feelings no more.

Death is senseless and has no regrets for what lives it may take, for death acts with purpose and with purpose there is reason.

I am the dreamer of dreams, but even in dreams, death exists.

Death is inevitable, death is life no more.

When I sleep, I am dead to the world, but alive inside.

I am immobile, I can't move, but I can dream.

So, in death do I dream, or does death dream of me?

I stare into the hollow eyes of death day in and day out, sunup to sundown all while its blade is pressed firm to my throat.

Death is what you fear.

I fear death no more.

# Losing Brothers

The hill I climb is much too steep.

The concrete is brittle and breaks beneath my feet.

My brothers beside me are falling back, falling toward a jagged bottom with no way back. Releasing lock of hand for silly sin and giving up early because there's no hope to win.

I hear a rip in the neck of my shirt, I found I was falling too, been falling since birth.

Lucky me; I managed to snag a branch but from this view, I can see the horrors of the avalanche. Bodies stacked up beneath me, piling higher and higher, climbing to reach me.

I'm losing brothers to drugs, to vices.

I'm losing brothers to gangs, to violence.

I'm losing brothers to hate, to fear.

I'm losing brothers to justice, promised but unclear.

So many are gone, my support beams are broken.

I struggle from where I hang, my collar is constricting and choking.

## Chapter 3: Anguish

This white-collar, it grows tighter the more I fight.

My hands pull the collar away from my neck, I pull with all my might.

I fight to breathe, I fight to be free because I feel as though I'm being lynched, as more death plummets around me.

How is it we've come so far but so many have reached their end?

It's like I'm losing all my brothers because we won't give in.

As I hang here, I know we must continue to be strong.

My dearest brothers open your eyes and please grab on.

## Not Enough Tears

There's emptiness in my life today, a soaking somber amongst the cold burning air.

It's dry and crisp, the texture of sand.

My eyes remained open through the searing silent night.

I escaped the cousin of death, they who left their mark.

An atmosphere which reeked of a dark presence whom did not leave me alone.

Through my bloodline, death quiets another, leaving me to wonder; how many more will be taken into the deep?

I have not enough tears to mourn them all.

This lake runs dry and death was my drought.

I am a desert walking on its hands and knees.

I can't get a break, not even a moment.

My life be spared, but my family be its feast.

Emotions boil high, the water must overflow.

## Chapter 3: Anguish

However, I have not enough tears to express the full extent of my sorrow.

My heart promised not to wail in the wind but how can I not?

Living is my blessing but a friendship with death is my curse.

I have not enough tears for all who've been slain.

Because I barely have enough tears for my own name.

# Withering Pride

All men have a certain amount of pride.

A precious vial of dignity we carry inside.

It keeps us, it is our brother's keeper.

Take this from him and what be left but ether.

A shapeless cut out of what is thought a man is supposed to be.

A man who is not unholy but holey.

When pride withers, men wither with pride.

Whimpering fatally in their failure, mocked to death by time.

I have come to the misfortune of encountering such defeat.

It holds me warm with mother's embrace, 'tis only my own deceit.

Is this the life of men, visions that narrow and dreams that shorten?

Ambitions abolished and all of life's meaning orphaned?

Without a vial to drink from, I drown in drunk.

## Chapter 3: Anguish

I fold without a fight because I am not the one.

I was once too proud, too powerful to lose.

This man has fallen to pieces and cannot be repaired with simple glue.

I am unworthy of my phallic symbol for I am a man who's limp.

My pride has withered with it but not my suicidal attempts.

What is there to live for when a man's essence is crushed?

My pride has withered away and I along with the dust.

# Attempted Murder

Attempted murder just about sums it up.

I was in denial, secretly I wanted to put on trial.

Every decision I made was as calculated as a PhD, and with each step I was closer to committing murder in the 1st degree.

## BANG!

Just like that.

In a life filled with infinite choices, my choice almost ended something you can't get back.

I took a step into the fire and became the inferno.

I laid in the dark and became one with the abyss.

The blaze grew too big and needed to be extinguished.

The void spread too far and needed to be diminished.

Although they are significant to my life, it was imperative this person be killed.

Body dropped, placed in a coffin box and sealed.

This was attempted murder, premeditated thought.

## Chapter 3: Anguish

The plan was perfect, no one would see it coming, a part of me didn't even think I'd get caught.

I stared into the mirror and my reflection stared back.

Eyes wide, I placed the gun against his head because I'm sick of the image.

This was not a suicide, not even close, and I didn't warn you because I knew you'd oppose.

No, there was nothing anyone could do to help.

I committed this murder because simply...I was unhappy with myself.

# Deceiver

My reality relies on R.E.M.

Dreams are truths, consciousness, fiction.

It is fact I was born into a dream, when I sleep, I awake.

For, my dreams are often more real than life.

It is why my lies are written into legacy.

The differences become construed and the lies become beacons for truth unyielding.

A waft of foul stench, fact's diluted form.

I am a deceiver, moving faster than the mind and outwitting the eyes with calm pulse.

I am as unnoticed as a mild gust weaving through a maze of falling leaves.

Within my solace, I have bridged a gap between two worlds.

While those still resting struggle to grasp one, I have become freed from binding chains in confusion.

Skating this thin ice of an illusion.

Falling firmly into fusion.

## Chapter 3: Anguish

Contriving stories that can make a believer out of the Devil.

A deceiver deceiving deception itself because the words I speak are sound.

A life led boundless and therefore real.

Extended beyond logic, passed the fostering of proper knowledge.

Could it be that I've fallen too deep?

Is it possible that I have deceived myself?

Are my dreams really real or a fallacy in my perception?

Is my life real or have I been living another deception?

# My War

It's hard to believe, I'd wish not to say but my war is my life each and every day.

For me, it is a battle, another fight to get through.

My fate may be in God's hands, but have you ever felt as though God forgets you?

I have, and it hurts to think.

Especially when you're alone and nearing the brink.

I was given this life, and its mine to protect but sometimes I give up and it's my body I neglect.

Everyone is my enemy; trust is not an option.

The world is without air and people hunger for my oxygen.

Love is the color of a blind man's sight.

He may see a rainbow but can never describe its might.

Ravens live alone and I flock as a loner.

A lone wolf in the forest, no pack and no owner.

I write my own passage, exiled in eternity.

*Chapter 3: Anguish*

Only the knowledge of coming death is what I want for certainty.

This is my war; my gun shall always be armed.

I am paranoid and even my own shadow is warned.

Do not think in error, I will not bow down and perish.

I crave power, I desire life, winning I cherish.

The art of war perfected and I apply to my life.

I will stand and conquer, quietly overcoming my strife.

This is my war, a place ruled silently.

I fight against the darkness in a subliminally controlled society.

# Without Answers

'Twas not the darkest of days nor was it the brightest.

Days were grey tears, grey rain, rain delivered from subtle pain.

It was nevertheless, nor the greater, so what would you have me do?

How do I heal what I cannot see?

I climb to the highest towers throwing words into an endless expanse.

I wait like a widow for some answer to return from the sea, but I am only greeted by answers that purposely deceive me.

'Twas not the darkest of days nor was it the brightest.

Days were grey tears, grey rain, rain delivered from subtle pain.

It was nevertheless, nor the greater, so what would you have me do?

Drain the blood from this open wound?

## Chapter 3: Anguish

Without the healing of the soul from inner self, these days would grow darker and the light ever so brighter and without those answers, I'd be lost.

# This Mad World

This is a mad world and I am a mad man.

Mad that the poles of the world were flipped.

Mad that somehow, right and wrong were switched.

Misaligned, scoliosis down billions of spines.

Crooked crooks drowning innocent minds.

Begging the question; when did the world become so blind?

Why does the world lay passive to such egregious crimes?

The sky blue became unnaturally black, her lungs inhaled our poisons until she couldn't get her sun back.

Fires surged through the great plains and many trees fell to sacrifice.

Man, bred too many great gains, and those great Danes fell to their insatiable appetite.

Water still, it is ill as it is filled with oozing trash; and why you ask?

Because the laziness of man.

## Chapter 3: Anguish

Men who refuse to change, refuse to lead and pave a better way.

To be selfless instead of selfish and cowering behind green veils.

Planning and plotting with their legally tender hands, prepared to strike me down when I finally take a stand.

This is a mad world and I am a mad man.

Does anyone see our child being taken in a white van?

No. We clock in and we clock out, living off scraps from day to day.

All work, and more work...never any inconsequential time to play.

No wonder so many hope it all comes crashing down.

It feels like this great land has oppressed us firmly to the ground.

Our muffled cries feeding the smiles of greedy men, we must choose to suffer or become one of them.

I am a mad man, and this is a mad world.

Books are traded for guns, violence and killing is fun.

Here's a line from the new national anthem, *"war is the only way for all of our daughters and sons."*

We gave it all to them, financed it with our trust.

We the people were the power and we sold them the power of us.

A power that comes from deep, the pure power of choice.

This is why I'm so mad because we gave up the power of our voice.

The world we live in has always been a maddening pyramid promising life at its peak.

But the promise is a lie because you see, the base is weak.

The controllers control the controlled, and the controlled allow the controllers to plunder and one day when the peak is all that is left, the controllers will be left to wonder, "*where did we go wrong, what ever happened to Earths song?*"

I imagine after that; our demise wouldn't be long.

This is a mad world; nothing makes any sense.

The world has less value than man-made cents.

I cringe to think that it is to money we've all surrendered.

## Chapter 3: Anguish

What a mad world we live in, what destruction we've delivered.

Something needs to change; what have we become?

If you don't do it, then sadly...I believe no one will be the one.

# Death with Mortal Eyes

I am here and I am now.

The maker of my choice the creator of my fate.

I am here and I am now.

The valley of death owes me no favor.

I have walked its bowels and I have felt its scorn.

I've been shown the blackness that would be my end yet spared by the angels' rod of what could have been my undoing.

I still tremble at the thought of it but always accept it when it comes.

I fear the moment of occurrence, however, calm in its presence.

It is then death looked to me with mortal eyes.

Empathy felt in emptiness.

I am here and I am now.

The maker of my choice, the creator of my fate.

I am here and I am now.

## Chapter 3: Anguish

Such roads I've taken to place me at this point.

Although I am bloody, I remain unbowed.

I cannot be upset for this is the line I have drawn.

I lead myself here and will make good of this life till I am gone.

I won't lie of the terror in dying but comfort me so as into the valley I tread.

Then death looked to me with mortal eyes.

I am here and I am now.

The maker of my choice, the creator of my fate,

I am here and I am now.

It is like death knew me all too well.

History shared in understanding.

Another day to be born, a blessing.

My head bloody and still unbowed.

It grows colder and I afraid, but I am ready to cross either gate.

Then death looked to me with mortal eyes.

I am here and I am now.

The maker of my choice, the creator of my fate.

I am here and I am now.

Shallow it feels as if it was yesterday.

I am reminded still in subtle ways.

I can never forget what could have been but wasn't.

My final days frozen in coffin.

Wood broken by my hand.

I can never surrender and yet I am grateful.

Such empathy felt in emptiness.

I will never forget as I am always reminded when death looks at me with mortal eyes.

Chapter 3: Anguish

# *Lurking Shadows*

Tonight, was the night I should have died.

Tonight, was the night the shadows that followed behind, came to light, glowing from a moon, the eye in the sky, spelling my name in the glimmering stars above.

Tonight, was the night death told me, that in the end, I will stand beside him when my heart pumps its lasting words given unto me by God and upon his pale horse we shall ride, ushering in new ages and tides.

Death told me on this night of unforgotten truth, that shadows lurk behind me, waiting for the chance to pull and yank me under.

Tonight, was the night the world turned at a faster pace.

Time became irrelevant and this very moment pertained to no matter of state.

This moment was empty, dismal and dark but this blackout had a light at the end of its tunnel. Smaller than a pinprick, but it was this light I could see.

Tonight, was the night Death was supposed to show me to my grave; the sickle he held was supposed to end it all.

However, this light amongst darkness which flowed through me for a moment in irrelevant time made me immortal, a creature whom disagreed with Death.

Tonight, I believe my might impressed Death, who now, before my time, stands with me, not against me until my true un-lasting breath.

I walk the light and lurk the shadows.

There is only your future, your fate, your destiny...accept it.

## Chapter 3: Anguish

# Forms of Evil

Liquid flowing forever formless, evil is just the same.

Emanating around us, it is right there in front of us.

It could even be standing beside you or perhaps, it's inside you.

Speaking softly, conjuring the worst of thoughts and fears.

It is the cause with no justice, the Saint Nick of your tears.

Light sucked from souls; pulsating life brought forth to bare no fruit.

Black ink on black letters, liquid black tsunamis and ash weather.

Evil in its vast forms has conquered the world.

It is the monster whom only killed the oyster for its pearl.

Green with envy, a demonic feeding frenzy.

A beast who does not want you to know its plight.

So, it waits to strangle you in your sleep at night.

Playing in your dreams while wearing a mask.

You're distracted, no longer able to recognize evil's tasks.

Anything human is not alien too me, so I too can be evil.

Evil whom takes many forms, its favorite form being people.

*Chapter 3: Anguish*

# *Faceless*

I am faceless, the man with no face.

I belong nowhere, I am without place.

You need not know my history; my past shall remain dead.

White walls once pure are splattered in red.
Love hath forsaken me, darkness becoming silencing.
Words no longer spoken; I've fallen victim to such travesty.

This is a world of shadows and a part of no land.

I belong nowhere; because I am the faceless man.

# Cluttered Mind

I am lost in a forest.

Tangled in the confines of needle weeds, lost in the questioning of cleaning.

Where to begin straightening up a once-tidy room?

Days of youthful purity have passed and with each passing second, waste is dumped atop my land.

Every vine I latch to is like a thorn into tender hand.

Ivy constricting and seething of poison.

Trash piling, a foul stench filling my head.

The higher I climb, the more jumbled my jungle in metaphor becomes.

I am scared as I go, marks that will stain me for a lifetime.

Absent of tomorrow and lacking the suns light of yesterday.

Vulgarities clamor, obstructing any personal ability to think.

Lost in a crowd of noise, I shrink.

Fare thee well, vibrant sparks upon stems implode.

Such misery in stillness and diminishing consciousness.

Time hath turned emotion to blank fields.

I am lost in a forest, still thick of needled weeds.

Junk continuously pushing through open pores.

Piercing me until I've succumbed.

Self-destructing shelves upon shelves of vile books.

Redacting this cluttered mind.

I've been taught now.

Filter tainted water.

Drink profoundly evaporated wisdom.

Inhale the steam for its messages of clarity.

Sift amongst the sludge and turn the sludge into beauty.

It doesn't matter where we begin, so long as we clean our cluttered minds.

# In Memory of Butterflies

Butterflies...I remember butterflies.

A meadow and the scent of summer poppies.

If I focus, I can hear the call of wild birds and feel the warmth of final sunsets glow.

Oh, and how can I forget, how can I forget the taste of blood as it pooled, cemented and became my lipstick?

See, I was bound and gagged with a black bag, beaten until blistered and brought to a place where I could be systematically censored.

The field was the last freedom I will ever know.

It is the birth and death of butterflies.

Where those with honeyed words could pollinate.

Where flowers were free because that was the true land of opportunity.

But this; this is four walls with bars, I believe they call it "the box".

A place where the cattle was herded and led to believe the barn was permanently locked.

## Chapter 3: Anguish

Their mission?

To breed butterflies of blind in order to prevent an up rise.

Surprise!

We didn't see the trap, and those who came before us tried exposing their act.

In fact, keep your eyes on the horizon, sometimes it's the only way to know the difference between lies and lion.

Trust me, they will deceive you.

Ask you to turn your back to the beast only to have the beast then end you.

The silencing of lambs, our beautiful speech hindered.

I was brought to a place where I could be systematically censored.

Now, here I am.

Uttering my truth to stonewall because if my words ever escaped, I'd be tongue-tied and hung, strung from a noose and swung.

My fluttering wings stripped from my body like this air is choked out of my lungs.

Hear me.

Sing your song of freedom even if only the trees are listening because these devils will do anything to keep the wise from outwardly speaking.

We were forced into this cage, handed a script and told to read it and just like the rest, I am forced to unwillingly repeat it.

However, I will never stop dreaming of golden fields.

My will, will continue its attempts to break this seal because memories...I have memories.

Red and vibrant, I was born in the valley of artists.

Where imaginations ran wild amongst the poppies and flowers.

If I focus, I can hear the call of wild birds and feel the warmth of final sunsets glow.

Oh, and butterflies...I will always remember butterflies and the fields where anything could grow.

Chapter 3: Anguish

# Media in White

I cannot help but feel angry inside as turmoil turns and boils, bubbling up and out of me.

I am a performer, an actor, and I am free.

At least so I think.

My emotions and imaginations have been gagged inside, trapped with a lion in which hungers but has been told to hide.

My wings' width rivals that of a condor, but they've been folded and clipped, and I wonder; what for?

Inside of me is a love suppressed, a caged beast, a force with desires to expand and express.

However, the stage in which I walk seems to be constructed with a narrow path.

I am given a mask and asked to wear a face, and upon it is written, "a minority's place".

As the clock ticks forward, I swell with fury as my eyes gather truth while watching these movies.

Scattered across the scene in light, the images come out primarily in white.

My people subdued to secondary positions.

Commonly used to laugh at, we are subjected to abuse, stereotyped or carefully crafted.

We rarely play the, hero and if were not at least a villain, then the film probably has zero.

It's not fair, as the scales tip in unbalance and I fear that this is being done with sheer malice.

Feeling as though I am judged based upon my color and I cannot express enough in words how hurt I am from being smothered.

I am an actor, infinite in what I can do.

Besides my own talent, I should have nothing else to prove.

I am more than my ethnicity; I am more than my skin.

I am more than my culture and the body I was born in.

This is a land that should have media in colors, a screen we should share equally with each other.

Not focusing on the bias side of history, narrowing the gap for others quite literally.

The youth needs to see more positive imagery because some of these depictions damage them subliminally.

As actors, we are limitless; challenge me.

Quit trying to conform a body to your ideology.

I have something greater erupting from deep inside.

A wave which follows no rules and no tide.

A lion who is sick and tired of being told to hide.

So, today we invent new stories that abide by no laws.

With paintbrushes, we gather, adding more and more colors of leaves autumn's fall.

A media in white should be a blank canvas for us all.

# -ism

This land is not your land, it belongs not to me or anyone.

We, merely children at play upon the unconditional kiss of our earth mother.

It is not your race that divides you, it is your mind.

Cry blood with me brother, see the world in red and maybe then you will understand.

The only ones who will die on this battlefield are of man.

*Chapter 3: Anguish*

# His Hands

I will call him Adam.

Simple man seduced by serpent to do awful things.

Tempted by ruby red apple, lush with life, he sought to draw me in sharing poisoning bite. Elegantly speaking promises of worldly things, appeasing the desperation internally for chasing a dream.

Lost in this rat race, I tried closing my eyes.

I tried traveling my thoughts, trying to believe any lie.

**His** hands were coarse and felt of razors.

**His** hands scarred deep, staining devil's mark in dark places.

**His** hands burned with sin as I burned in troubled waters.

**His** hands sought to pull me away from self and innocent hollers.

What am I worth?

I stood bare, weighing the weight of my mortality at this moment.

Disgusted by the thought of signing Lucifer's contract, giving up my own fate with purity for uncertainty of wealth and things.

My stomach churned like butter in a barrel, as the spiders crawled over me.

Ears were pierced by the sound of my crying body.

Agony is real, my home is invaded by the unwanted.

The surface of me bombed in bombardment.

**His** hands were cruel and cared not for mine.

**His** hands destroyed a painting of beautiful signs.

**His** hands ripped apart the fabric of my reality.

**His** hands treated fellow life as meat and not humanity.

Call him Adam.

A part of me created from his rib.

Resisting the horrors, I too am capable to give.

I left because nothing good would arise from this evil in such men.

Sometimes I hate to entertain the thought that I even have such kin.

We are worth a value in priceless.

## Chapter 3: Anguish

Drifting upon a leaf falling with fallen skies.

Sell not the most valuable possession venerable to the sly.

Speak up and speak out.

Do not allow them to trap you in the night.

Do not fall asleep for demons, stay up and fight.

**His** hands were dirty, but mine remained clean.

**His** hands attempted to kill, but mine gave sight to the unseen.

**His** hands occupied a space, one I cannot forget.

**His** hands did not beat me, the lesson was forgive.

# Addiction

My body yearns for the sweet taste of it.

Begging me, pleading me for more in greed.

Touching the places I moan, teething the places I tickle.

It taunts me, baiting me on because I'm addicted.

Heart rate surges blood, my skin now flush.

Hairs stand on end and I can feel the slightest tremor.

Saliva pools in my palette but I feel dead of thirst.

My body reminds me of this euphoria I lust.

It is clawing and scratching in the back of my mind.

Knocking and tapping my skull, raping my thoughts, raping my logic, raping my will to choose.

I don't want it but my body it intrudes.

Fucking me with cruel intentions.

I plead and I plead with the word; no.

But it insists on thrusting harder with the word; YES!

As morality fades and I give way to addiction.

## Chapter 3: Anguish

This scourge has been weighed.

I can't carry it, so it is crushing.

I default the wisest decision for partial gratification.

Placing self in harm's way and there is no justification.

Except, that I am addicted, and it haunts me.

Demonic shadow creeping and crawling behind me.

I am addicted, do you understand my agony?

That these tears I shed are not because I'm imprisoned.

These tears I shed are because I can't get a fix.

My body is not of my own or at least one I control.

I'm addicted to being addicted passionately. Always desiring more.

Yet, I am strong and will not falter.

I am large and my craving smaller.

But this battle has been waged and so it continues.

I am terminally addicted.

How about you, what's on your menu?

# A Conversation

Hey!

                                            Hey.

What's on your mind?

                              A lot and nothing.

Yeah?

                                          Yeah.

It's like that sometimes.

                        It's like that for me often.

Oh?

                   Yeah, and it's only getting worse.

I'm sure you'll figure out a way to quiet your mind eventually.

          We'll see. It's pretty adamant about what it
                                                    wants.

If it'll help, why not?

                                    Because it won't.

I see.

## Chapter 3: Anguish

> I need to stay strong.

I believe in you.

> Thanks, but...I've already given in once to fend off the feeling.

I know, I was there.

> Why did I do that!?

You did whatever you had to do.

> Then why do I feel so bad about it?

I don't know; there's nothing to be ashamed of.

> I hope you're right.

Of course, I am. I'm you.

> That's what I'm afraid of.

Afraid because I'm you?

> No, afraid that you think you're right when you're actually wrong.

We.

> What?

Afraid that We think We're right.

> Shut up.

Sure, once you give me more of what I want.

                                      Whose side are you on?

Always yours and whichever side you choose.

                                          Sincerely, me.

*With love, you.*

*Chapter 3: Anguish*

# Generation Ωmega

We are of the world's end.

Torn from cloth, we burn of blood, content in this place pretend.

We imagine it water, although it mud, biding our time drowning in drugs.

Twist of leaf and we believe its freedom, as time, it passes, and we are swept under rug.

No longer dust but merely humans without reason, without purpose, thus we die, decaying in our own defecated filth.

We have lost the will to rise.

Yet, still find the will to kill.

Moving ever so swiftly to the graveyard.

We slowly lose the will to live.

Like empty clocks, our brains stop ticking.

They have become still, and we have stopped thinking.

Force fed by tube, we intake what is given.

Not to be digested, only simply eaten.

Pyramids pierce skies with unobtainable peaks.

Nutrients soaked from the land, but none of it leaks.

Stench foul breaks wind against our nose tips but we remain stagnant, pillared amongst cadavers and crows hiss.

We believe we cannot exist without amounts.

Imaginary numbers for imaginary accounts.

Delighting in lies and torture of soul.

We sit back and wait as disease takes its toll.

Worship not the modern world as some do Mecca.

We are of the world's end, this is generation

# Ωmega.

*Chapter 3: Anguish*

# *Fallen Stars*

The sky is falling; it's falling so fast.

Rain of light molten blaze plummet.

This is the end of our spinning film reel.

I loved the sky and treasured it dearly.

Now the sun surrounded by neighboring stars, stare down upon me with punishing heat.

Burning delicate skin because of heinous sin.

Bending the steel rods which once were my support, keeping a heavy head held high and marveled at what dreams stretched across the Milky Way.

Until one by one, the stars fell.

Those who made wishes, became victim to solar flare.

Solar winds carried death through air.

The sky burned red; the clouds grew dark.

Our moon melted away listening for an angel's harp.

Earth was bludgeoned and scarred deep past its crust.

The core then spewed its liquids out onto the surface.

Oceans fluid with lava.

Life as we know it just wasted away.

Eons in the making, destroyed in seconds.

Erased from the pages in time, pulled right from under us.

I never thought I'd see the day, the sanctuary we called home would collide into aster.

It is now I guess we join our fellow fallen stars in this universal dance of flames.

*Chapter 3: Anguish*

# The Section That Night Covers

Not all and everything is drenched in light of holy sun.

There are underworlds of sewage, alleys of excrement and filth.

There are places in disdain, much darker than others, and then there is the section that night covers.

It is a way away, shadowed from a lonely star.

A place so dark, light cannot flow in or out, around or through.

It is a place of smog and in it you are smothered, and then there is the section that night covers. There are places where their eyes are not their eyes because they are machine's; manufactured, fabricated and taught.

You may not even be you; not even your thoughts.

A world filled with puppets who ruckus over dead lovers, and then there is the section that night covers.

Deep into the slums, further down, past the rats and the bums.

Crawling into the darkness where your eyes cannot adjust.

Here, are the forgotten ones.

Here, is the coldest place you could ever know, and then there is the section that night covers.

A section life did not give to.

A section where even life forgets you.

Its caverns filled with despair from above and an ocean of tears splashing against the barren walls, and then there is the section that night covers.

From where I'm standing, I can see the lie I dreamt of escaping.

The matrix within a web, it's so amazing.

Look around you, can you see it, the undiscovered?

We've been in it this whole time...this is the section that night covers.

## Sickness

Ill and inhabited by some creature, it strips me of such simple life.

Gnawing at my fabric, it weakens tightly sewn tissues, leaving me to cling to what freedoms I have left.

Soon to be bedridden, aching and weary, here I will experience what I am sure will be like my dying day.

Coughing, wheezing; my nose has a broken gasket.

Freezing, burning; my brain snapped a fuse.

My body apparently is confused, dealing with so many genetically altered things.

My body no longer knows what to do and even doctors today don't have a clue.

On the brighter side, for once it's not a lie when I call in sick.

I can kick back and relax and hopefully heal quick.

Today is my day, a day I don't get too often.

A day of rest, sleep and Oxycontin.

I can only wait until this war which wages subsides as cells, bacteria and viruses collide.

Annoyed that such tiny things can cause great immeasurable hindrance, that any man should be humbled and fear the power of his sickness.

Chapter 3: Anguish

# *We Walk a Thin Line*

Let me go, let me free!

Can't you see these chains and shackles that contain and bound me?

Bound me to a solid line we abide by.

Blind and pacing forth into darkness.

Like a world consumed in the ideals of global golden arches.

Always paranoid, living in absolute fear.

Waiting, anticipating for the number you hold to be called because the judges sentencing is near.

Heaven or hell, forever you could dwell, black as a raven lost in Nevermore.

So, I scream in the dark, speaking the devil's game, hoping you hear my outpour.

We are hanging by strings on a stage that death plays.

Controlled by a master like a puppet, it controls many ways.

While we balance on a thin line, blind, and in the dark.

We are forced forward never knowing when we will be stripped apart.

Ignorance is bliss; at least this is what it wishes us to believe.

Without great knowledge, and wisdom, our souls are easily retrieved.

Find the signs, open your eyes and see truth.

Stop giving into false wine; it is not thee blood, be it juice.

You are on a list of dead and death seeks for you.

It will take your hand and I say give it much ado.

It doesn't have to be our time, we can fight it, we can live.

Don't fall into deaths traps, never fall, never give in.

Get off the line; break the cuffs around your ankles and wrists!

Run liberated in the dark pits of mist shouting.

Say, "Let me go, let me free, I can see the timeline you've set for me!"

All can't be saved, but I can say this; It's not my time to go.

## Chapter 3: Anguish

My heart will keep on beating and stop on its own.

I do not need death's blade to bring my inevitable fate.

Don't let the zigzagging lines go straight.

**Beep**

**Beep**

**Beep**

**Flatline** _____

# Hatred Dream

Embroidered into the concave of my skull is trauma triggered.

Anger boiled from immense heat radiating from this tragedy.

Uncontrolled, this calamity drenches dreams until I suffocate.

Gasping for air like the red blood cells I am dying with.

So, I claw and break nails from fingertips in desperate escape.

Withering like a fish out of water and while the land dries, I with it.

Hell rises to surface as the ground blisters and bubbles.

Gurgling screams pierce rupturing eardrums.

I am consumed by this rapture.

Sand under pressure transforms into glass, glass into mirror and I stare in horror at what truth is revealed.

The bodies I stand upon, mere victims of my rage.

Ravens gather to feast and prey upon this plate.

*Chapter 3: Anguish*

I wish not to become this evil I now radiate but the blackness of ravens calls for me to satiate endless, vengeful hunger I cannot set aside.

Irate, my eyes swear allegiance to fury and flames I abide.

I am the darkness; I am the hate.

I am my own hell and I will cross the Devils gate.

# Beggar's Story

I am the face of mankind, but a face mankind is ashamed of.

I am the arms of the world but arms the world breaks.

I am the story untold; I am the truth in shadow.

This is the beggar's story.

A tale of tales woven into urban streets under streetlights, colored tents and sewers beneath, a tale coursing through veins and fleshy membranes as toxins provide for escape.

We are the judgeless, enduring harsh judgment and not from any God, but man.

Suffering scrutiny instead of love, we are the outcast of society.

Innocent and without a savior's sanctuary, we are wrought with more grief than grace.

Men would rather see us euthanized than saved; we are like animals without a face, easily treated like scum, rodents, or pigeons.

## Chapter 3: Anguish

Freedom is still a prison, as I am beaten by verbally abusive people and my regretted decisions.

I am the body of nations, but a body nation's abuse.

I am the legs of cities, but legs a city refuses to use.

I am the story untold; I am the truth in shadow.

This is the beggar's story.

I beg because admittedly I am unable.

I plea because unfortunately, I am incapable.

Scared for what has yet to come, I am lost and without a way.

Today I was mocked, laughed at and scorned.

I wasn't lifted up, I was pushed down upon piss stench of concrete and dragged, dragged through the filth developed by my peers.

I shuddered at their grins, content while living in this disgusting evil.

I say, I would rather remain needy than live a life shared amongst the greedy for most of the world is poor and only a few are with plenty.

I am the issue of humanity, but an issue humanity refuses to solve.

I am the picture of the people, but a picture the people pretend not to see.

I am the story untold; I am the truth in shadow.

This is the beggar's story.

When a man speaks, *"There will always be poor,"* he is a man trying to protect his own wealth.

When a man speaks, *"There is little to nothing we can do,"* he is a man bound by fear, afraid to acknowledge the scope of possibilities because it is beyond human and therefore Godlike.

It is only man who cowers and proposes something is impossible.

It is only man who is frightened by the thought of something greater than himself.

It is only man who cannot accept not knowing the unknown.

I whisper for spare change, I look for only bread, I thirst for simple drink, and it's I you dread.

I am sorry if I am angry, rude or disrespectful.

I am sorry if I am odd and at times unpleasant.

## Chapter 3: Anguish

Please understand it's because I am cold and frightened too.

I have nowhere to sleep, do you?

This is a story untold, a story that is millenniums old.

I am the truth in shadow, the beggar in plain sight.

Die for me as I have died for you, following the light.

# Grandfather Clock

And so, I am father time.

Father to my timeline as you parent to yours.

But not so apparent is this dying score.

Melodic and soft, it begins and ends.

Vibrations of song cease before ears can taste and it is replaced by something distant and unsettling.

Too far for my time to see, but perhaps, just maybe, a part of me will.

Until then, we set fire and burn amongst urban decay.

*Chapter 3: Anguish*

# Blackest Book of Apathy

In my twisted hands, I possess holy words of pain.

Conjured from the deepest scars, these words sincerely defame.

The cover, bound by flesh, is my charred and burning skin.

Apathy placed in center; each chapter is made of my sin.

Now gather around as I tell the true tales splintered from frowning faces and dead with complexion pale.

Opening the blackest book of apathy, is coffin with final nail.

Pandora's box released death without a flowing sail.

Witches and ghosts, demons and possessed hosts, scour the world to place hands around throats and choke.

Listen for the coyote, it howls at the red light.

Fear the bear and snake while they feast on the blood moon night.

Soulless as a robot, the city will burn.

I will bring these monsters to life and watch the universe turn.

Dark woods will consume, and we shall haunt the masses.

The darkest days are fast approaching, you will not outlast us.

Beholden to me is the blackest book of apathy, ordained by father time, death and all its majesty.

Welcome to the magic, where we are nothing left.

Faceless, we are the end, we are the final breath.

Chapter 3: Anguish

# *My Darkness*

Into the darkness that is me.

I am not helpless, but still, I cannot see.

I am not helpless, but still, I cannot speak.

I am not helpless, but still, I cannot feel.

I am not helpless, but still, I cannot heal.

So, further, I go into the darkness.

Swallowed by the sin that is me.

## *It Is You I Live Through*

They say, everything happens for a reason.

Every second, every minute of every hour.

Moments imbued with this sentiment.

Buried under choices upon choices of unclaimed sediment.

The reason may be foreign and feel unfamiliar.

The answer could appear absent and any meaning muted.

However still, we continue forward, a drift along currents of air.

Paper airplanes put a loft the lungs of life and somehow, someway, I found my way to you. Everything happens for a reason.

Even long goodbyes.

You never see it coming, being left alone to cry.

Hold fast, could it be so, the possibility of finding you.

The answer, the meaning, the truth.

Although I am gone, it is you I live through.

## Chapter 3: Anguish

Your smile, your spirit, your grace.

The bridge between here and after.

Your heart keeps me alive and our memories safe.

We met for so many reasons, one was to set me free.

Knowing I can pass without fear, because of the love you gave me.

I lived a life worth living, I had you by my side.

Now it is you I live through until we meet at the end of time.

# Reminisce a Younger Me

I look at the old me and I see a young man excited about his future to be.

I look at the me today and I see an old man cynical and bitter about what used to be.

What could have been?
So often from somewhere deep inside of me, I wanna have hope, I wanna be free.

But in my experience, I've been beaten down, now all I see is this fate and me a prisoner to it.

I wonder, how can I get back to being the younger me?

The young man who was fearless and could clearly see.

How can I be...me?

Instead of this bitter hag, this wrinkled rag.

A man who shoots down his own dreams.

I often wonder how I can get back to just being me.

I need to figure it out, I need to walk a different route because before I know it, I'll be gone.

Although in truth, I already died so long ago.

*Chapter 3: Anguish*

# *Confused*

The world is ill-prepared.

Its ignorance and its fear leaves me alone with this confusion.

Restraining me from loving me completely.

I am a mistake; I am a monster.

I should be hung; I should be drowned.

My own blood is upon me.

Leviticus strike so with truth.

Cut away the fat from my flesh.

Kill the abomination sprawled out before you.

There are no answers, mouths sewn shut.

Discovery of my definition is up to me and me alone.

Lost in limbo between identities.

I am as misunderstood as the world misunderstands.

It is through your clouded eyes I am unhappy.

# Becoming the Comparison

I'm sick and tired of the selfie.

No one seems to understand the cost of the self fee.

I walked away because I heard my soul say help me.

Then I realized my soul was so unhealthy.

I was chasing the lives of the insta wealthy.

Emulating fitness models like Chelsea or Kelsey.

My life was worthless unless I could sell me.

So, I fabricated a life to appear compelling.

Tell me; what's more smelly?

Pretending I've been to New Delhi?

Or breath fresh from eating old veggies?

Hint, hint; the lie should be telling.

Aiding in the death of well-being.

Empathy of self is now seeing.

You are no longer a person...just a thing.

An object not meant to be heard...just seen.

In other words, we've become an abstract of nothing.

Nothing but the most filthy, ego driven, self-prophesying, *"I live in front of my camera, I'm the one who built me, I did it on my own and look at my Bentley, the only value in life is having plenty and if you aint on my level, then you aint with me"* kind of person.

So, I'll hang myself from this soapbox because one thing is very clear.

My life is unimportant to post; therefore, I must not belong here.

# I Am My Own Worst Enemy

I woke up today.

My feet planted firmly on the ground.

Looked myself in the mirror and said; today is the day you'll be unbound.

Unbound from your vices, unbound from your hurt, unbound from your crisis and unbound from your dirt.

I went to church today.

My knees dug into the hardwood.

With hands folded in prayer I said; today is the day you'll forgive.

Forgive me for my shortcomings, forgive me for my sin, forgive me for my worst follies and forgive me for what might have been.

I went back home today.

A metal tip pressed firmly against my temple.

With a finger on a trigger they said; today is the day you'll be freed.

## Chapter 3: Anguish

Freed from your body, freed from your ache, freed from what's on you and freed from your mistakes.

I looked them in the eyes.

My best friend betraying me.

A loud crack and a flash, ending my entire legacy.

Saw myself in the mirror, so much I wanted to say.

But then again, it's too late, I wanted it this way.

# Nothing

This is it.

It is simple.

As blank as this page was.

Emptiness made unemptied.

Simply because I made words.

Yet, still, the page is void.

These words ultimately mean nothing.

Existing only because I thought them.

Remaining because you thought you saw them.

This is it.

It is simple.

There is and will only ever be nothing.

Nothing is always there.

Nothing hasn't gone anywhere.

Something is just an illusion.

A product of nothing itself.

## Chapter 3: Anguish

Nothing is infinite.

And we...merely poetry on a page.

Erase it.

# Over, River the Nile

"Please come with me,

let's go away, over, river the Nile.

Please come with me,

let's go away, over, river the Nile."

Today I find comfort in one man's song.

I listen closely as I search for home.

In my travels, he guides me, providing the strength to carry on or soothing melody in sleepless nights until the moon has gone.

We were displaced by gunfire; our village was desecrated.

The man and I now nomads, walking the trails as ill-fated.

He sings aloud, tails of a better place.

He sings of a land without judgment or earthly trace.

It goes...

"Please come with me,

## Chapter 3: Anguish

let's go away, over, river the Nile.

Please come with me,

let's go away, over, river the Nile."

Africa, oh Africa, you are my mother and I am your child.

Centered on a map as my heart is centered in my chest.

You pulse for this earth, and from it, life came to birth.

So, I don't understand why they defile your face?

It pains these youthful eyes, eyes whom lost their innocence.

Tears forced back and I, overtaken by vengeance.

Having to throw my anger to the sky because I cannot direct it.

There are so many guilty hands involved, even I have become infected.

Hate, I begin to hate.

Wondering why, why hasn't any of this been resolved?

And then he sings...

"Please come with me,

let's go away, over, river the Nile.

Please come with me,

let's go away, over, river the Nile."

See, life is harsh here; our world is like the savanna.

Predator's hunt for prey and the prey, pray for salvation.

Our queen is raped by the world, robbed of her natural wealth.

They take and they take until she is left with a dry and sandy well.

Rivers run black as oil is sucked from her pours.

The land no longer shines, her diamonds have been gorged.

Listen, our motherland is becoming silent.

More and more poachers trade flesh with violence.

Her children are dying from war, famine, disease and for what?

But nothing.

My feet blister as we migrate, my lips splitting and cracking from thirst.

## Chapter 3: Anguish

From the dunes in the Sahara, to the vast jungles of the Congo.

My land has been washed in blood.

Even the skies billow red ribbons that run.

For, all over my country, I can hear their song.

All over my country, you can hear us all.

We sing...

"Please come with me,

let's go away, over, river the Nile.

Please come with me,

let's go away, over, river the Nile."

Alas, I have made it.

The river flowing as though crystals were its content.

The man across the way, beckoning for me to cross it.

I look back to bid my mother farewell.

In her place, I can see the pillaging of a town.

The flames so familiar, the smoke and voices that echo.

Further from the river I go, closer to this pain I can feel.

The man who sings is dead and suddenly I remember how he was killed.

Rebels stormed my home; I was left draining red on the floor.

He picked me up and held me to his bosom, as more rebels stormed through the burning door.

He sang...

"Please come with me,

let's go away, over, river the Nile.

Please come with me,

let's go away, over, river the Nile."

His words my final comfort in this land I call my home.

Ravaged and scarred by war I was an orphan, but not alone. Many of us disassembled or dismembered will leave behind violets to be remembered. It is to you that finds them whom my soul will remain kindred.
Knowing now the truth, I can leave you Mother Africa.

Calling from across the river for your children to find us.

Follow our voice, see the land beyond what is being taken

## Chapter 3: Anguish

and listen for the song of the man and child.

Together we sing...

"Please come with me,

let's go away, over, river the Nile.

Please come with me,

let's go away, over, river the Nile."

# Just Another Brother

I knew you would come for me if I climbed too far.

Because a brother with wealth and a brother with power.

A brother who is loved and a brother who is admired.

Is a brother who is feared, envied, hated and sought to be devoured.

I knew you would come for me; I was warned this is how it would be.

The oppressor applying pressure to keep my head from rising.

To keep me from closing my two eyes and opening a third.

Finding the word and asking what is the truth?

For after more than 400 years of physical and systemic abuse.

I wonder, how could I ever get ahead when you'd decapitate me in my youth?

Seriously...what's the use, when all you want to do is see me swinging from a noose.

*Chapter 3: Anguish*

Muthafucka, you would do anything to see me lose, wouldn't you!?

Nothing but a bunch of fools.

Tell me!

Do you really hate the color of my skin that much?

That you'd kill the righteous one, taking a stand at the front of the bus, sitting there in that seat, for each and every one of us?

Damn...I knew you'd come for me.

The touch of death is present and I, willfully unexpectant.

I hope you know, the "hood" you wear will not hide the killer underneath.

But what hurts the most, is it had to be just another brother from the streets.

It pains me to fear you, a fellow king, another black man like me.

A pain so torturous in all this time; I hate to admit it...but I'm starting to agree.

Like crabs in a bucket...~~nigga,~~ are we?

Because if that's the case...now I see.

My dearest brother, we ain't never been freed.

Because the realest slavery has been between **You** & **Me**.

# IF OPRAH COULD HEAR MY WORDS

CHAPTER 4 OF 5

# BLISS

THIS CHAPTER IS ABOUT BLISS.

IT IS FREEDOM AND IT IS JOY.

LIFE IN THE MOMENT.

A BOUNTIFUL SOUL.

WAITING TO BE DISCOVERED.

EXPERIENCED AND SHARED.

IT IS ME.

## Solis

If Oprah could hear my words, she would know I am a man written in bliss.

Written in the ways a smile tells a story words fail to describe, or the way joy feels as it dances inside.

If Oprah could hear my words, she would hear a voice looking to share splendor.

A man sharing the fabric of life, holding it not for himself.

Instead, he hands it to everyone else; for what is the universe if not a smile itself?

If Oprah could hear my words, she would know I am a man written in bliss.

A poem meant to shape eyes and curve arms into warm embraces.

Heal all ailments under the boom and cheer of glee.

Lift Atlas on these shoulders and let the world be free.

If Oprah could hear my words, she would hear the words of a man who knows his place here.

A man who understands that we are the watchers.

We see the universe and the universe sees us.

If Oprah could hear my words, she would know we carry identical names, we are all pieces of illustrated poetry and we are all beautifully framed.

It is what ties us to everything, I believe it is our fate.

We are all bliss, we are the same, we are the human race.

*Chapter 4: Bliss*

# 5MEO

I lay back into the ether.

Gone be the sounds, gone be the lights, gone be the sensations, gone be my life.

There is just me.

I am nothing and at the same time, I am everything.

The past, the passing present & the future.

All there was, is, or will ever be.

From it, I rise.

From the ether, I rise.

I am now.

I am the answer.

In life, and in death.

I am free.

Always.

I am free.

# Women and the Happiness of Men

A man by nature, through his eyes, is drawn by physical.

The sway in her hips, the soft curve drawn upon breast and butt, the pulsing pucker in lips or bat of eyes.

A man is drawn like a fly to warm light, for it is women that give a man's life such joy.

Women, the illustrious deities that illuminate and brighten such hollow shells of men.

It is for women that men are strong.

However, women are also what men are weak for.

Their gentle caress of hand, their moist kiss against skin or cheek, their bodies entwining, senses delighting in partake of romance.

A man melts like an ice cube left on a sizzling stovetop, left in the mercy of woman's love.

It seems that almost everything men do is quite simply to impress you.

It is funny how much alike the birds we can act too.

Without women, men admittedly would fall apart because women are the reason why some men even have a sweetheart.

Women give life to child as well as give life to man.

It is for women that men even have the courage to stand.

Men may be from Mars, and women from Venus, but one thing's for certain; men are willing to travel the distance between us.

A man is drawn to a woman naturally because it is for women men can truly live happily.

# 6-String Guitar

My hands ache, they tremble, the muscles squeeze and cramp.

My fingertips blistered and sore, the skin peels and breaks.

I close my eyes and wipe sweat from brow.

Adjust pick in hand, then strum in G, and what rings out is beyond peace for me.

My 6-string guitar starts singing.

Notes and tones vibrant in airwaves, gathering into a cacophony of acoustic symphony, bouncing off walls, moving time and space around me.

It is at this moment in musical solitude I find harmony.

Whether harmonious I play or pluck into apathy, my outlet is spoken six strings at a time.

E, A, D, G, B, E; an equation for creating infinity.

Statements and more statements that will be stated.

Song by song because history fated to all guitarists who wield distorted hand, whom played without giving up due to the wrath of man.

## Chapter 4: Bliss

It is easy to become angry at the difficulties and quit when overwhelmed by impatience.

But I accept, with love such a flaw, if just for these brief moments I can play.

Enduring binding and twisting, stretching and curling, nearly breaking and ripping my hand apart.

Only for passion of the magic in music.

One string at a time, six in total, with pick between fingertips, I solo and strum.

From it, dance sounds unwinding my mind in ways so profound.

Six strings lost in music; it is peace I have found.

*Dedicated to*

*~ Grandpa Stan*

*Rest in Melodic Peace*

# The Quest of a Passionate Flower

I was on my way to the bus stop and along my path chirped a tiny flower.

It asked if I could carry it and blushed red in excitement.

I said, why not?

Take my hand and quest we shall.

Such beauty in today should be shared with a friend and pal.

Away we went, from green stem ruby, I plucked.

It laughed with joy as we swept through air.

Today was tranquil, unexplainable peace.

The flower and I could feel the still vibrations in electricity.

Tension dispelled, eased muscles limp without motion.

Mental state absent in thought, we levitated from conscious and into a deeper focus.

## Chapter 4: Bliss

It is in this moment golden gates give, and locks break open.

Inpouring light from divine setting our souls free amongst the ocean.

Time elapses but we do not notice.

No longer a flower in palm, now lay lotus.

Our chariot arrives, galloping in, as we are pulled to the back of the bus by gravities whim.

As I sit, alongside me stares a man.

His aura is broken, his pain outspoken.

From the cracks in his white lips, slips a question, "*What made you take that flower?*"

I declared, It was passion, the flower was red with passion!

The man smiled and dropped his head and said, "*I was once passionate too.*

*I asked about the flower because it's something I used to do.*

*But that was long ago when my world was brand new.*"

The flower looked at me and smiled as if it found its destiny.

The quest it longed for, fated just ahead of me.

I said, I want you to have this to remind you of such passion you possess.

The beauty in this flower is red within your breast.

He took the flower, which once again bloomed into lotus.

He then told a story held within and it was burning.

His tears ran clear, as did mine.

Our souls had briefly placed a stop on time.

Bitten by addiction he has suffered so much.

Then he said to me, *"This is the first time I haven't thought of drugs in months."*

He tucked the flower neatly under his bracelet.

New hope twinkled in his eye and I believed he could make it.

We came to the point in history where all part ways.

Then he took my hand and spoke, *"Listen, I do believe I met an angel today.*

*We were meant to meet; you've shown me the way.*

*I want you to know that your passion is tried and true.*

## Chapter 4: Bliss

*So, before I go, I want to say, thank you."*

The sunset fell behind the horizon as I continued on home.

I couldn't help but think how all occurs with reason.

The flower on this day and the man on the bus, all compounding into one greater meaning.

Passion, it is red as the blood which flows in veins.

It is the nectar from the flowers we drink.

Passion is the language of our souls, the secrets shared in connection.

Passion is never lost, and it never goes.

Simply live your life and pick up a rose.

# Reading My Book

I sit upon a chair, staring into these eyes that curve and loop in endless ways.

Dripping, running off both sides of this face that scares me but only wants to take me to a far, far away place.

I devise a plan to gather information from these inscriptions, codecs marked completely over every layer, internally.

Somehow writings burned further than this cover, seeping onto a page like hieroglyphs, they stain inside a temple.

Megaliths and monuments priceless to the hands that erected them from the nothingness of scratch.

Could it be my life is too chaotic?

Maybe my focus is directed to the clouds, airborne and adrift.

Sailing a sea floating from a face with many more things to say other than the pitter-patter, drip drop of day to day.

## Chapter 4: Bliss

Do I need to escape away from reality before escaping further into fantasy; falling in love in such solitude romantically?

Recluse I recline, settling in until comfortable.

Clear I remain, buoyant, mentally bobbing about.

Eyes poised to page; I begin a journey.

Silence, quiet, calm down, relax, shush...I'm reading my book.

# Dare I Lust for Derrière

Before I begin, I apologize...I don't mean to offend.

I must confess, I have a problem...I love women's rear ends.

You have to understand this love is more than some sick perverse want of man.

I swear it's embedded in my brain like some natural submersed plan.

See, men are like primal beasts with large egos but a lady's behind can turn men into complete heroes.

Or even melt hearts at temperatures of absolute zero.

Every step is explosive, detonating my brain into commotion, my eyes recording and watching every motion.

Only a woman can move like the ocean.

Beauty so profound it can't be described when spoken because the geometry involved means it had to be written in some complex form deeper than surface, to explain how perfect her caboose is.

## Chapter 4: Bliss

Do I dare stare at her derrière; marvel at the roundness standing there?

Stunned and asking this question; embarrassed of this powerful obsession, wanting to worship a woman's curvaceous blessing without guilt, shame, or stressing.

Ladies!

Your backsides are persuading.

Convincing us to do the dumb things we do daily.

Divinity sculpted lady, not only to give birth to baby but change the ways of men.

Because by having you in our lives is the one way, we all win.

I know it sounds shallow.

There's no way to explain it; a woman's butt creates emotions and it's impossible to contain it.

So, let me say I'm sorry for the guys who let it show in the worst way…but damn.

It's so invigorating when I see you from the back view.

I swear!

If you proposed right now, I'd jump and say; I do!

Only a fool wouldn't marry you and the lucky one that does, better love and respect you.

He better praise those buttery biscuits God blessed behind you.

Because when those buns rise, they turn my sky blue and it's crazy to me that some think the booty is taboo.

<u>But</u> believe you me; it is a dream come true and I couldn't think of anything better to be addicted to.

I speak for all men when I say; women everywhere, stride with pride!

You are our masters; may your butts be our guide.

*Chapter 4: Bliss*

# *All the World's a Stage*

I am but a mere vestige in a mountain of truth, the laughing face of smile or depression turned away.

I am shadows of lights blocked by impervious figures, or truth denied by morals and society's shame.

I am the love in passion, boiling of sex and eroticism, home of hate, bleeding of anger in antagonist kiss.

I am tears fought from falling, a story wrought with grief, masked by penciled-in joy, wavered by an eraser's belief.

This is not a body of lies, only genuine emotion.

A fabricated jacket Gods refuse to wear with devotion.

I am but a mere glint in a universe of stars, the diary revealing pages meant to be burned upon death.

I am words kept buried under layers of flesh.

I am an actor created, an open vessel or severed vein promised to purge fact upon floor in undeniable stain.

Evaporating all I know and understand so it is to escape me.

I will fill such a void with truth so profound it leaves the audience shaking.

I am an actor and all the world is my stage.

Truthfulness, my story, conveyed to those willing to listen.

I am the teller of tales, capable of nothing but truth from the minds it was given.

I am a performer, individually breathing a bridging gap, taking hands and showing them dreams untold, marveled by what is real and unfolding.

I am but mere truth unheard in a clamor of lies.

I am an actor; I am the voice of many lives.

# *Poetry*

Phonically packaged to pacifically personify philosophies of people and phenomenal paintings, printed on paper poetry, moves with pace, visually presenting a palace in pattern on page.

Poets can pantomime through lips, perplexing perspectives, passionately providing panoramic views of pacifism and peace, as I pencil a pact in paragraph, praying this paradise is perennial, pensive of periodic pain placed within peripheral.

Perhaps such problems profane are procured for us to perjure, for poetry provides the population with a portal for human outpour.

Optimum outlets of oratory octets, overtly opening ears like an overture in opera, off-springing opinions, and rights to objection, organizing oddities and bringing ordinary to obscurity, outright outrageous or outstanding for the occasion.

Optically it could be just the mirage of an oasis.

Otherwise, it's an ocean organic in omen, ornately orthodox to deliver origins of oath that poetry is like an organ obtained by the omnipotent, orchestral in our minds, becoming omniscient.

Entering Earth empty, we are educated, edited and sealed in an envelope addressed to eternity, eclipsed in ebony, falling from edge into the epic epicenter, engulfed by an enigma endless in its eccentric enchantment, effortlessly emitting emotions elicit in electricity, eager to embody the embryo, endowing envisions efficient in element, enough to heal entire epidemics with exceptional elixir, engaging an event etched by ethereal energy, evoking euphoric entities to eradicate evil enemies into exodus.

Taste the tale that poets tell through teeth that teach theory with tender technique, tantalizing thinkers who are thrilled by tangents talked.

Take time to hear testimony transmitted via telepathy, using telekinesis to tear tectonics.

With poems, I tease, translating theatre, I try to tame tenacious thieves, taking things for tabloids, tailoring taint upon totems, speaking terribly while I am striking tableau on table.

## Chapter 4: Bliss

Words are my talismans so I can stand against tall tanks.

Like trees with tact, I thunder over topography maps for the land is my throne.

Rap and R&B rhythm with poetry; a radiant recipe, reaching in a room, ready to rock and roll ravens, rouse and ready risqué recipients for ragtime rule, as I remind reality of my repertoire, and we rejoice along rushing river's Rhapsody, rippling and rotating on a ride I refuse to relinquish, reading romantic romances ripe with wedded ring's resolution of the righteous raising rebellion in reckoning.

Remarkable how poetry recognizes all races, reinforcing releasing of hate because real love cannot be replaced.

Young of youthful lore we yell, yearning for gardens to flow of flowering yards, yellow of sun, yodeling in song of yesterday, yielding the yarn to the yahoo yelping, surfing on a yacht limber like yoga, ignoring yammer from yawning yokel's, because yenta festers like yogurt, yet we rise like yeast and under heavy winds, we yaw, measuring with yardsticks the good times in yearbooks yearly, and yes, this is my signature, alliteration in illustrating poetry.

## That's My Jam

Turn it up because that's my jam.

Music flowing through me in a rhythm unplanned.

It is my meditation.

I elevate into a new plane.

Existing on new lands in new lanes.

A sound ringing in hymn for every occasion.

Touching every complex emotion and station.

Invading with vibrations and euphoric persuasions.

I move with the music with unadulterated elation.

Turn it up because that's my jam.

A melody so magnificent I can't help but clap my hands.

Reaching down inside of me pulling out ancient feelings.

Jolting me back to my roots of primal beginnings.

Instruments collaborating in a cult I'd gladly join.

Cultivating creations of sound to get the earth going.

# Chapter 4: Bliss

**Turning volume to the point where speakers go BAM!**

**When the right song comes on, turn it up because that's my jam.**

# Family Tree

I love my family with a strawberry heart.

Apple red and full of life, it shimmers from the cuff of my sleeve.

Radiant like sun, my light bounces upon leaves. Feeding rich history as I marvel at the miracle that is me.

You could not begin to imagine the extraordinary journey, traveled and trailed, succeeded and failed to grow my family tree.

Origin unknown, yet seed planted deep.

It starved for light and the will to breathe.

It burrowed through earth with might, eventually breaking free.

This tree sprouted into green and kept on growing.

The branches reached towards the heavens, standing with its canopy in cumulus clouds.

The trunk as wide as a continent, swallowing the planet in shadow with a cooling shroud.

From starting seed, to its many rings and the leaves that flourish, I am connected by sap.

## Chapter 4: Bliss

My family tree survived, eventually bearing fruit to me.

Therefore, I dig at the roots of us to set your story free.

Honoring the many leaves that withered and have fallen.

Mourning loss but celebrating our families will to keep going.

I love my family with all of my heart, my family is the reason I am even here from the start.

Thank you, ancestors, for enduring unimaginable hardships.

I am lucky to be connected to this timeline, placing my markings.

So, my children and their children can see; we are who we are because of the strength and love in nectar.

Passed down through the veins in our family tree together.

# *Looking for Adventure*

I incubate in a shell waiting to break free from it as if a turtle.

Sprinting for the ocean on beach full of danger, I hurdle.

Vessels pinch tightly as I see a vast horizon.

Taking trident in attempt to call Poseidon.

Let the ocean speak and carry me away.

I long for the world's openness, she dares me to play.

Looking for adventure, I aim to travel the world abound.

As a sea turtle in the waters, it is adventure I have found.

Trapped in a cage waiting to break free from it as if a bird.

I flutter about as much as I can to feel wind stir.

Arms outstretched; I daydream of flight.

Exploring unknowns and anyplace of my delight.

Hear my song, notes buzzing and clipping in air.

I long for the skies and the clouds up there.

Looking for adventure, I aim to fly the world around.

As a bird in the sky, it is adventure I have found.

Bustling in a cocoon waiting to break free from it as if a butterfly.

I fantasize what it will be like to have wings glowing in sun like firefly.

Decorated in design by journeys I have already explored as a caterpillar.

Inching my way slowly to destination, earning my marks in thriller.

Breaking my form down to nothing except baring soul.

I long to reform, morph, taking to life in radiant star's glow.

Looking for adventure, I aim to taste the treasure of sweet nectar around.

As a butterfly amongst flowers, it is adventure I have found.

# A Supper for One

*Food*...a word as delicious as it sounds, indicating thoughts to spark and moisten my palette.

Bubbling belly awakening beast in gurgling gut, I salaciously desire to savor the flavor of buffet.

The smorgasbord of glutens galore, I need sustenance of fork and knives.

As tongue hangs from mouth drooling like dog, I can only think of smothering myself in plate like a hog.

Sweets and sours, tangy or bitter, leaves and red meat, my mouth is open like a capital F, seeking to devour two bowls of O's until nothing's left, leaving me to look like a capital D, messy and unkempt.

I quiver as I think of lapping tasty morsel; the pleasure I receive digesting such a delicacy, taking into me an aphrodisiac of ecstasy.

This is a supper for one; check please!

*Chapter 4: Bliss*

# Hiss of Snake and Letter X

I am serpent and she is my target.

X marks the spot of where I shall bite.

Sinking my fangs into the flesh of her soul.

The taste of her body and wine I expose.

I am drunk from the glass of her, as my venom intoxicates.

Hear me hiss as I wrap around tightly.

Binding body to body, I coil with passion.

Jaws open and she I intake.

Tasting the letter X, for she is my favorite.

# Pedal to The Metal

When life becomes too much and I feel out of control, I strap into the driver's seat, turn the key and let go.

With pedal to the metal and rubber burning atop concrete and pavement.

Adrenaline surges into my veins as the speed increase insanely.

The seatbelt squeezes against my expanding and collapsing chest.

Windows are rolled down and I vanish between the door and seat crevice.

Cool air wisps around the cockpit, caressing my flushed face.

My nerves tense as my need for speed begs me to build in pace.

Although only miles per hour, I attempt to break Mach speeds.

I want to move faster than sound and escape everything.

## Chapter 4: Bliss

Many do not see this moment; they fear going past one hundred.

But speed demons leave trails of fire leading a path to this gate rarely wandered.

However, first, one must learn to shift and change gear.

Take hold of their life and control the ride while in a swerve or sudden veer.

My fingers tight around the steering wheel, I speed on the open plain.

I watch the lines streak past like filmstrips down the long straightaway.

I'll vanish without a trace or even a track left on the road.

It is here in my driver's seat where I am free to roam.

Nothing here can reach me, I am now moving faster than sound.

When I am driving, I can achieve the impossible because I am liberated and now unbound.

# *A Simple Dream*

When I close my eyes at night and dream, one fantasy is pulled from stream.

That before life should see its end, mankind could forgive and make amends.

Because Shakespeare's saddest tragedy is the one about the waste of human potential.

A story written and unfinished because even he knew obtaining such bliss is not simple.

We know the answer is love; my question is, why do so many fear it?

Fear the cozy grace of warmth, they'd rather not go near it.

So, love we sing and sing we must.

Tempting souls out of the cold and away from the dusk.

I see a world where good news is looked upon how bad news is today.

A eutopia where death is not a man-made sentence based on where you lay.

I see a better world.

## Chapter 4: Bliss

If the sun is Apollo, then we are his laurel.

We are so much more than we see.

We aren't even half of what we could be.

# Her Hands

I will call her Eve.

Complex woman made from the broken pieces of my rib.

She understands trotted upon soul in ways much deeper than my own.

Where I can be irreverent, allowing fire to thrash with scolding heat; she is the water who can calm and cause such blaze to cease.

They are a part of me, a mirrored reflection of all I stand to be.

The beast, wild and untamed.

I am held under control by the angel who wields my reins.

**Her** hands were soft and always welcoming.

**Her** hands healed the wounds profusely bleeding.

**Her** hands kissed my body into turbulent tremor.

**Her** hands brought salvation to Earth.

What am I worth?

## Chapter 4: Bliss

Only the entire weight of her world.

We are balanced, like equal weights on ship.

Ballast, we stabilize and come to shore wrought with chaos.

She keeps me grounded for my head always seeks the sun.

One day I'll arrive to the moon, but for now, she's my only one.

The feel of her touch against the skin of my own is priceless.

I'd beg to live twice only to experience these moments.

**Her** hands were the bed I rested on.

**Her** hands I'd even confess my evils too.

**Her** hands liberated me from the darkness I manifested.

**Her** hands gifted to me by some savior.

Call her Eve.

She is the comfort of my dreams when reality is more than I can stomach.

She is the purity that life has lost.

Eve was not tricked; man was tricked.

Man toyed with Eden and locked himself from paradise and Eve is paradise; heaven in all its splendor.

I know this by her touch.

She is blossoming fruit and is thy forbidden tree.

Man disobeyed his father's order, but through her, I am now free.

**Her** hands were pure as I continue to drink from the waters.

**Her** hands gave life to flesh thought to be lifeless.

**Her** hands bearing the pain no man wishes to carry.

**Her** hands brought life into creation.

*Chapter 4: Bliss*

# A Greater Bond

I can't explain this connection, but we are like moon bringing in tides.

Vanquishing the hardships of today and conquering fates of tomorrow.

Through their eyes, I am faced without judgment nor do I judge them.

Every moment we share is love in purest form; it is the love between friends.

> **If a look is worth a thousand words, all else have but a penny.**
>
> **Because words without sound are louder than any.**
>
> **To the outside, it seems we speak a language unknown.**
>
> **Instead of mere verse, our feelings are shown.**
>
> **Still, waters run deep, two minds, one heart.**
>
> **To one drum we beat and are never apart.**

I don't believe in one soulmate; such a promise should be shared.

*One may obtain the heart of life-long lover, but what of the heart of life-long friend?*

*This world war waged cannot be won alone; there are lessons to be learned and lessons to be sought.*

*I will better you and you will better me; fighting the scourging flames together despite how bleak.*

> **You've shown me a path that I don't yet fully comprehend.**
>
> **I know in my heart I've finally found a true friend.**
>
> **Our eternal sun, it burns so bright.**
>
> **You feel my warmth, as I see your light.**
>
> **I have longed for a union as beautiful as such.**
>
> **I admire your passion and you've taught me so much.**

*Inside jokes and the adventures we have.*

*The secrets we've locked from the mischief we've had.*

*Our lives are like journals, a beautiful diary written together.*

*Privacy kept hidden, like these words I fail to express.*

*I trust you so much; in my skeleton, I'd say you're my ribs.*

*Protecting my vitals from harm, you encourage me to live.*

*Could it be we are soil grounded as one?*

*It is only with my friend I could delight in unworldly fun.*

**Delight doesn't begin to describe the joy I feel inside.**

**To be your true self with another is all one could really ask for, ever.**

**Like the earth that abounds, it is our nature so wild and so free.**

**The fruit is our trust, I believe in you, and you in me.**

*It's uncanny, how they can just about...*

**...finish their sentences or understand their thoughts without words.**

*We rise together and we fall together; we float atop feathers in air.*

**We breathe with heavy winds and fly without care.**

**You see, what we share in common is much more than any song; our souls are of the universe.**

**We are friends of a greater bond.**

Chapter 4: Bliss

# The Good Life

There is not a dollar to my name, but I am still living the good life.

No, I don't have a mansion in the hills with a view, but my body is healthy, and my eyes are too.

No, I don't have a fancy car or a private jet, but I am grateful for my legs.

I am blessed with every step.

Strangers don't chase after me begging for my autograph.

The paparazzi doesn't bombard me with blinding photographs.

I'm not in magazines or plastered on countless billboards and yet, I am still living the good life.

Nothing can replace the look on their face when I come home.

My family may be strange, but I am not alone.

I play in the yard with siblings, awed by how they've grown.

The only autograph they need is my love youthfully shown.

Hearts warmed in the priceless joys of laughter.

Friends and our pictures, embarrassing moments caught with regret soon after.

Riddle me with snapshots and our wonderful lives together.

The only paparazzi I need are my friends capturing real moments forever.

You can find me in a wallet and other times a purse.

My picture can be found anywhere my love has lurked.

No, I'm not famous, I'm not a celebrity star.

My life is not glorified by riches or land conquered by war.

I am not a politician, I am not a corporate C.E.O.

However, my world is still wonderful, my world glows.

So much to be thankful for, every day I wear a smile.

This tiny heart still beats innocent as a child.

My wealth is a measure many wish to achieve.

They are sadly fooled by an ideal that deceives.

There is not a dollar to my name and honestly, I could care less.

## Chapter 4: Bliss

**Why? Because I'm doing what I love to do and still living the good life.**

# Rain Falls

I am looking from the inside out, and the world through my eyes is grey.

The air is so crisp, when I inhale, phlegm retreats from the frost and my lungs open like parting valleys.

Cooling chills skate along my sloping spine and I shiver from the breeze under darkening clouds as anvils enshroud blue skies; swallowing what remains of daybreak.

Pillows soaked from the heavy of grief, soar overhead and finally break.

The first tear bursts upon the ground and I watch as the rain falls.

Each drop a tidal wave crashing down on me, soon building into a flood fleeting across my flesh.

I am consumed in a shower of rainfall, consumed in the downpour of eyes.

I am looking from the outside in, and the person through my eyes is grey.

I can see what pain they carry and through thick mud, they trudge, weighed down by burden.

## Chapter 4: Bliss

The pressure from fearing a lightning strike.

Reservoirs hold water bottled up inside.

The damn refuses to give way, they refuse to cry.

Emotions swell and blacken above in soul's heaven.

Blood chills and frozen air blows between vessels.

Hurt is consumed by the person, held deep in the collapsing frame of me.

Looking from the inside out, I run into the rainfall.

I open my arms and scream.

The water cascades over my face and in my mind, I cry; the tears I can't produce rain and finally fall from my eyes.

I am looking from the outside in, I can see steam rise from the waterfall.

Negative energy released in explosive rage pours through pores, pouring into the rain which soothes me.

Rainfall, tears for when I have none to shed, providing security in its touch and tenderness in purity.

Rainfall, breathing life when life has been dehydrated of me, squeezing out impurities like bitterness expelled from lemon.

Rainfall, a time to dance, a time to sing and a time to play, learn to embrace the storms, reveling in their majesty.

Because inside out or outside in, pain will come and pain will go, but release the tears inside and free yourself in rainfall.

Chapter 4: Bliss

# *Letter of Forgiveness*

I write this to you, the last brother I wish not to lose.

Hoping you can finally listen through my letter of forgiveness.

My older brother could have had a life, but life misaimed fortune and gave his up for mine. Leaving you to pick up the mantle as the eldest in my eyes.

Such confusion in dark times, trust, I dare not speak.

However still, somehow, we bonded as brothers, much further than some seek.

Teaching me as mother did to keep smiling and show teeth.

Outside, life can be tragic, but love radiates underneath.

We were not of blood, more of brothers than your own and despite despairs looming, I knew I'd be not alone.

So, I write this to you, the last brother I wish not to lose.

Hoping, you can finally listen through my letter of forgiveness.

I grew like mighty redwood rooted in fertile earth.

Born from angelic womb and raised to be mighty from birth.

I considered you my blood brother through thick and worse.

Looked for you whenever I could, we put each other first.

Then you disappeared during a time I needed you most, the fury inside me became a deadly cancer and I its host.

Grand Daddy passes, not long after Granny does too.

I was left with a pain and wondering where the hell were you?

The weight of it all, at that age I couldn't handle.

Suppressed, then it ignited when I discovered you were taken guilty as vandal. So, I write this to you, the last brother I wish not to lose.

Hoping, you can finally listen through my letter of forgiveness.

Here me true, I apologize to the river Rio Grande, I lost another brother to the oceans and the sand.

All of this hurt, it's not the same without your brother's hand.

## Chapter 4: Bliss

I had learn to fall and bruise but pick myself back up.

Nothing is promised to us, we create our own luck.

I wrote this letter before we die because we can't take anything back no matter how hard we try.

Tears can flood a storm, thunder can echo of cries, but if something were to happen, it'd be awful if we haven't said goodbye.

So, I write this to you, the last brother I wish not to lose.

Hoping, you can finally listen through my letter of forgiveness.

I hope to see you again one day, I miss our youth and how we'd all play.

Just know I love you, man, handle your business.

Do whatever it takes because we can fix this.

I hope I've made you proud more than ever now.

I speak for the family, we miss you, and I say that out loud.

I hate to be so personal, but I say this with reason.

I hope this letter reaches you safely while away in prison.

I wrote this for you, the last brother I wish not to lose.

Hoping, you hear me and finally listen.

I love you, brother; you are <u>eternally forgiven</u>.

*Chapter 4: Bliss*

# Social Networking

The future is here, and the future is now.

A click away and all day we play, interconnected on a digital highway.

The world is becoming smaller as we bond with technology.

Almost as if it was organically woven into our biology.

A profound insight; something I think we all have in common.

We are wrapped in the thought of communication by the push of a button.

Social networking attempts to tie the world into one, sewing oceans and binding shores together into a knot that can't be undone.

Bringing us closer while at the same time closing many doors.

We create avatars to live for us in a prospering community of sorts.

A new universe spawned with a new language.

Transforming our reality again and some thought this was dangerous.

I disagree, social networking is a personal journal or diary.

Revealing many a secret all of which keep me smiling.

We are all the same, feel the joy in the idea you're not alone.

With tears, laughs and all; we share the zone.

Every post proving how human we all are.

In this world, however cliché, we are all stars.

Social networking is the bonding of mankind.

A plea for acceptance in the human eyes.

It's an expulsion of inner reality unto a world with open arms.

We social network to share ourselves and hearts charm.

Yes, there are many opinions, and, in that chat, we can differ.

But *"imo"* I believe there is something greater we deliver.

Chapter 4: Bliss

Social networking is a portal binding our stretching land.

Social networking is a window into what it means to be human.

# Master Debater of Self & Self-Pleasure

Whoever said masturbation was bad had no respect for their self, because only you can please you like nobody else.

I discovered this trick when I was just a wee little boy.

Sitting in a bath full of bubbles bobbing, I discovered a new toy.

All I knew at that time was this sensation is incredible and if I touched myself enough, the end result was unforgettable.

I acted as if I found some unknown hidden secret, wondering if anyone knew what I knew and if they didn't, should I keep it?

Imagine my astonishment when I found out I wasn't the only one; it seems at that age we all had an instinct to grab our handguns.

A feeling reinforced when eyes first gaze a body that amazes us, arousing newly formed desires and introducing a blazing lust.

## Chapter 4: Bliss

This act was pure and in one explosive moment, my mind was clear.

I felt no shame and I wasn't weird.

However, there was a time I thought maybe masturbation was a sin, but that was back during that one time when my mom walked in.

I was sprawled out under a green blanket, occupied with a magazine and my mom opened the door without knocking, to see her son in a shocking scene.

She jumped and yelped, closing the door immediately, while I screamed in embarrassment, finishing up expediently.

Something so great now felt so wrong.

I felt dirty and I felt filthy as if I couldn't go on.

But to my surprise, my mom and I had a long talk.

I learned it was natural and made a request for room locks.

She denied my request, but I felt better about self-pleasuring.

Knowing that it's normal for men and women re-calculated my entire measuring.

Boys choke chickens and girls pet kittens.

There's nothing wrong with being self-smitten.

Clenching of toes and emphatic convulsions of muscles,

stimulating the brain with hormones and compulsives.

Goosebumps pout lips to shiver and quake unsteady.

The heart races upwards and breathing becomes heavy.

They say stress causes cancer, well, your hand could be the release.

I say get to work all day and set the bad energy free.

Whoever said masturbation was bad, had no respect for their self.

Because <u>only you</u> can <u>love you</u> like <u>nobody else</u>.

*Chapter 4: Bliss*

# Devouring Desire

I look at her and I am starving.

I am parched and within her, I wish to be drowning.

Her scent whisks me off my feet.

Cradled next to her my heart anxiously beats.

She lay before me; her naked vulnerability be my feast.

I was invited to prey upon flesh, she longs to satisfy this beast.

Quench the unquenchable, fill the unfillable.

Be it so, I take her hand.

Soft and supple, what warm and tender land.

Like bed, here I will place my head.

Close mine eyes and dream.

Oh...what a dream it will be.

Not a dream at all, but truest true, a dream come true.

A taste so sweet, like morning dew.

The due of life, the taste of another day to be lived.

A thrill, a rush, something only the fringe can give.

I am eager.

I leap from the edge to go deeper.

Parting gates, her fruits keeper and I am helpless.

Addicted now to the flavor, tempted by this behavior.

It gnaws at the nape of my neck.

Same as I yearn to bite the base of her...blessings.

What a wonderful vexing.

Honey sweet, I lick my lips to remember my favorite treat.

To whom I will always surrender.

She is desire.

Chapter 4: Bliss

# *In Pursuit of Destiny*

Between my reality and my fantasy, I am a dream.

I found two seams and crossed them.

Isn't that what life sometimes seems?

Two worlds crossed, two halves of one whole lost.

So, I, the dreamer of dreams take this brush and paint.

Paint violently the second half of one whole gone.

Spending a long life trying to achieve the impossible.

Expending my blood, every ounce.

Isn't that what it costs?

I live to die, and I die to live.

Doing so only in pursuit of the answer.

The answer to a dream, the answer to a destiny.

A clear moment I shall not fear.

See my wounds, a testament of my years.

My destiny's here.

Sufferings cure, I feel as though I've always known her.

I, the dreamer of dreams, take this brush and paint.

Paint with love the second half of one whole lost.

Spending a lifetime achieving what was always possible.

Spending all of me, every ounce.

A lifetime of faith for a moment of grace.

Isn't that what it costs?

Are we not compelled to follow the yellow road until we've arrived at Oz?

I, the dreamer of dreams exist to paint my own fantasy.

A dream that I devote the rest of me, so when I arrive, it can have the best of me.

Because in my heart I know this is God's test of me, to wake in the pursuit of my destiny.

# Ability of God

With brush and color, visions come to life.

Dreams are given animation unto gentle light.

Human soul rises, laid on canvases of thought.

Painters possess the eyes of God.

Bend and leap move with might.

Dance emotions into rhythm's sight.

Bass speaks deep into body and thought.

Dancers possess the limbs of God.

Truth rings out and man stops to self-reflect.

Reminding entities what it means to truly connect.

Emotions we fear yet are embraced in thought.

Actors possess the heart of God.

Culmination of diversity through vibrations of air.

Instruments of percussion horns and strings kiss ears with care.

Language in sound, connecting differences in thought.

Musicians possess the ears of God.

Beauty in vocals, angels birthed in song.

Bridge divinity among living things here and gone.

Vibrations in melody felt now and after in thought.

Singers possess the voice of God.

Formed in puzzle and released in story.

Invention of tale inspiring greater glory.

Tellers of folklore deliver belief and faith of thought.

Writer's possess the words of God.

We are capable of creating by imagining, our minds are open gates.

With thumbs, fingers, and palms, we can alter the fabric of space.

My mind is the universe and the universe my picture in thought.

We are artists who possess the abilities of God.

# This Present Moment

There is nothing more beautiful than right now.

While I sit atop a tarnished rock and gaze over the waters before me; a tree trunk breaches from the depths.

It spews a fountain of water and grabs hold the sunlight.

Paints its mist in rainbows and glows of sunshine.

Turtles of many peek their tiny heads above the surface to see, and many birds flock ashore to ensure they too are witnessing.

Or, perhaps I am wrong, perhaps it is just me.

A witness of the present moment, a witness of just being.

While I sit atop a tarnished rock, my ears pound from the sound of droplets crashing upon the water's edge.

My ears ring from the singing of birds, and their language chattering from bobbing of heads.

It is atop this rock, I sit, truly at peace.

Here and now, it is magic, I am at ease.

The water waves to me as each critter shares in its splendor.

Whenever the nectar of life was touched, a ripple was sent from the center.

Each ring expanding and colliding with another.

It seems as though every answer exists somewhere amongst her.

The fountain grew, I nothing more than a beast.

But I am wild in this moment, I am free.

A fractional part of a collective, the beauty of nature's symphony.

This fountain is God and I the only witness to its majesty.

Every second profound, every day without price.

I understand, I was birthed with the ultimate prize.

I am here and I am now.

I am living and I am alive.

I feel no fear because I saw the world now through God's eyes.

This wasn't an accident, nor was it a calculated plan.

*Chapter 4: Bliss*

We simply exist as both, balanced in life's hands.

The rainbow soon faded; the geyser eventually ceased.

The trunk returned to the deep as the sun slowly retreats.

Nothing is more beautiful than this present moment.

For in death there is light, and light is always now.

# Candid

Candid.

It is in these moments we are free.

Precious and small, minute and easily missed.

Here we are alive; here we can just be.

Candid.

Snapshots of humanity, snapshots of life.

Captured easily with an iris of camera,

but so easily missed by the naked eyes.

Candid.

Hold fast, take time and see.

Nothing is forever, except echoes of moments.

These tiny echoes we all share candidly.

*Chapter 4: Bliss*

# *Appreciate Your Real Self*

See me, the real me.

Unfiltered and not retouched.

No mutations not even make up.

Only me and the perfections that are my imperfections.

Made clear by the father sun, as I wilt away radiating beauty.

Beauty that is my own.

A love-hate that is my cross to bear

and on my back, I will carry that weight.

Hoist it up and be nailed to it.

Body bread, blood is wine.

This body is mine and it's beautiful!

# Strand

I know, I know…it's just a strand of her hair but let me tell you about the complexities and beauty found there. It is a treasure map, leading back to one of the single most powerful entities on earth. Her name is: woman and I marvel at her grandeur.

Chapter 4: Bliss

# Without a Phone

I didn't have my phone today and at first, I panicked.

I was anxious, and I was bored almost every other second.

Then something happened and of course, I didn't have my phone to capture it.

And as we all know...if it ain't a post, then there's no point in it even happening.

I felt as though my day was lingering.

As if the sun were a boulder being pushed through sand.

Time going nowhere.

Held there by the absoluteness of my boredom.

I am aware of it and I want to die.

I am aware of it and I...I am aware?

A sensation not lost but faded.

Surreal, this recognition of the moment.

Can I see?

Good God, I can still see!

I am still here for me.

Present in the awakening of my presence.

Remembering...ah yes, this is what it must be like.

To be.

Chapter 4: Bliss

# *Steady Drifting*

It's an early morning am, gotta thank the lord I'm livin.

Kickin on my socks and shoes, then the road I'll be hittin.

Stuck in traffic and late for work.

Carpool is tempting but with my luck, it's more trouble than it's worth.

I ain't stressing though, life is in the timing and God is in the wind.

So, my mind is in the clouds and I stay steady drifting.

Clocked into work but ain't really *"clocked in"*.

My body may be present, but my mind still wanderin.

A 9-5, my constant reminder that I am not defined by the job I do.

I am much more fresh than new.

I fall below absolute zero to the power of two...cool.

And a note...you may have my flesh, but you'll never have my soul.

I'll do what I have to do to survive, but my life is worth more than your goal.

You see me working, but trust, I am elsewhere.

Living in the holy power of daydreams, I am elsewhere.

Ear to my inner God and believe me I am listening.

Like a petal in the breeze, I stay steady drifting.

*Chapter 4: Bliss*

# Slumber

I knew you before, I'll know you after.

Through starry nights, even sunny days.

I give unto thee.

For moments at a time, under the weight of dreams.

You are the sands of birth and rebirth.

The teacher of death and surrender.

Hold me now.

Keep me for a time.

Hold me close, I am yours.

# Giving

I have nothing to give but I will give it to you anyway.

Even if it hurts me, I will give it to you anyway.

Because the greatest gift I could receive, is knowing I could play a part in making you happy.

And so...I have nothing to give, but I will give you what I can anyway.

*Chapter 4: Bliss*

# Can You Stand the Rain?

My new philosophy, please let it rain.

I wanna splash in the puddles playing kiddie games.

Dance like Gene Kelly cause I'm singing in the rain

and my only other worry; is this water going to stain?

I'm a grown-up kid.

Twirling in this downpour is where I live.

Jumping hurdle after hurdle, making leaps and bounds.

I'm leaping so high I never wanna come down.

It takes more work to frown than it does to smile.

So, I'm ear to ear and riding waves like a tidal.

Take a picture and if you catch me cheesing.

Know, rain or shine, it's good times and that's the reason.

I hear the thunder raging in the distance reaching out,

to the joys and the laughs that we thunder all about.

I say, let it rain, let it pour, let it bring more.

Let it cleanse this world, from our souls to the core.

# Sunshine

Creative combustible, I'm coming out the big bang.

My hands, man, God-given tools of a grand plan.

L - O - V - E, steaming roots of a green tree,

growing from my toes up to my wrinkled fingertips.

Teaching me to teach the peace that needs to be taught,

to the young heads thinking art needs to be bought.

Naw homie...the art is free.

Just say, *the sun is overly, but the sunshine is me.*

When I wake up, I wake up in the flow of paint.

With these words comes the pictures that I make.

Maybe some you'll get, maybe some you won't,

but the worth of expression is felt in its jolt.

Like the move of the currents through the flow of its people.

As we rise like the birds and perch the highest steeples.

Ripples of inspirations, creations of my mind.

So, I'll give it all to you because we make the sun rise.

*Chapter 4: Bliss*

# *Burn the Dark Clouds Away*

Today's the day and I'm feeling like El Sol.

¿Cual es tu nombre? The guy who makes the sky glow.

Forget my bad days, all those days are no good.

I took my info and learned like we all should.

I listen to poetry in the wind.

I make my mental note, speak it out, then send.

She makes me feel like I'm floating.

Up in a nimbus and over the world.

But still...the dark clouds roll in.

Dim days ahead but my heart stays open.

I'm chill...I keep pace with my arteries.

Every scar is etched onto my physical diary.

My sun is shining even when it's just the moon out and like a wolf,

I'm howling just to hear my crew shout.

Whatever the day, I'll share my love with you.

**Even if it's raining, keep on smiling your shine will get you through.**

*Chapter 4: Bliss*

# *Teddy Tie: A Lifelong Friend*

My bestest friend who need say not a word.

the keeper of my secrets and the bearer of needed truth.

The great endurer of my affliction and my healer too.

By my side always, sitting there with a smile.

They have comforted me, played with me.

All the while asking for nothing in return.

Through longest night I am protected.

By my shining knight in nightmares.

Through longest day I am nourished.

By my bountiful bear in barest lands.

They are more than just cotton what lies beneath is softest love.

My innocence, my childhood, most priceless treasures.

Laid with me at birth and laid with me at death.

Teddy Tie, a lifelong friend.

The guardian of my nest, my chaperone beyond final breath.

My teddy bear is simply the best.

# Happiness Through You

This is not a love poem.

Only a testament of how you make me feel.

The description is simple.

Intangible, and sought by all who know it.

Happiness.

I found it with you.

Truly content beyond dreams I fly.

I can say I'm happy and for the first time...mean it.

This is not a love poem.

Only a testament of how you make me feel, and language serves no justice here.

All I can say is.

Thank you.

Chapter 4: Bliss

# Home Again

I am a wayward traveler, lost in the deep of the outer wilds.

A drift along shimmering giants and tugged by some weak force.

It can be lonely in the vacant if not for myself.

My own voice my company, sometimes a stranger.

Adrift, blinded by so many lights and tugged by some weak force I am in motion and there is nothing to stop me.

Accelerate, set abound to a destination.

Dissolved piece by piece, emulsified into the nothing around me.

A child's laughter, my tiny footsteps along the floor.

Memories, my essence as I cross through each and every door.

I am here, I am everywhere, a peace known only in womb.

I am a wayward traveler sent out to find, lost in the mysteries of the outer wilds.

We...are...and tugged by some weak force.

Called into the arms of our mother, our father, of ourselves.

A peace only known in womb.

Where we long to be and guided by some weak force.

I am home again.

I am...home.

*Chapter 4: Bliss*

# Grateful

I cannot be a pessimist.

Because I am alive, and despite all its woes,

the greatest gift, regardless of length...

is life.

# IF OPRAH COULD HEAR MY WORDS

## CHAPTER 5 OF 5

# WISDOM

THIS CHAPTER IS ABOUT WISDOM.

IT IS ANCIENT AND BEYOND TIME.

INFINITE AS THE MIND.

EXPANDING THE SOUL.

WAITING TO BE AWAKENED.

BEGINNING AND END.

IT IS US.

### *Tertia Oculus*

It came to me in a dream, singular in thought.

We danced, we laughed, and we sang.

There it was; subtle tremor in my heart which grew too readily.

Forming constructs into words, before being blown from lips and exploding unto the silent air of absent ears.

So, we waltzed, and we moved until we became one.

Each dream like a star itself, each star reaching out like novae.

Wishing for touch, fantasies of hold, wanting to be heard amongst falling warm tears of dew. Like sweet rain pure in verb, sounds ripple and rush upon the ponds milky surface.

It is then I wondered if Oprah could hear my words.

I ask the expanse in between; do you carry such echoes of voice; can she hear the cry?

The howling of a wolf pleading under blue moon, hoping for his one chance and if she heard them; could she feel them too?

Because through the expanse I have felt her words and I hear them deeply.

As I have listened, I have grown and as I have felt, I am feeling.

My heart opened to wisdom and I stepping forth into being.

All this from one dream.

Singular in thought, of a power I cannot deny and the answer to my question is so very wise.

She has felt what we all have and knows only what is divinely true.

Our experience is shared, she is human just like me and just like you.

My mind now at ease, I could then only smile.

Another step into clarity as I meet the destiny, I have known all the while.

Here I go, stepping off the great cliff with faith in free falling into the wild.

Blessed by what measures such love has done, I am thankful to be Earths child.

Now my dreams are coming true, gifted to me from whom I am faithful.

The omnipotent, who brought life to hand placing written eyes into book.

This gift unto me, I can now share...I can now unfold with all of you.

Through the unknown in this Universe, through thought and through symphony.

We are all connected, we are all always listening.

# #Black

#Black is an interesting color.

We fear it.

#Black cats and #Black beasts.

#Black garments for Columbine shootings and #Black suits for funeral proceedings.

We tremble in #Black rooms absent of light and have nightmares when we close our eyes in blackest night.

#Black plague, #Black death, #Black is evil, even the Devil is kept in the blackest chest.

#Black, it is the absence of light, invisible and unseen.

I, however, am visible and can be seen.

Nor am I absent, I am a tangible thing.

Dawned with a color, I believe misrepresents, but if I am to wear it upon my skin then it should be known.

#Black, absorbing the light and reflecting none back.

Holding within me all there is and ever will be.

I am a star and beneath this #Black body exists a being of radiance.

#Black, it is truth and it is lies, it is life and it is death.

#Black is pain and #Black is pleasure.

#Black is fear, but to embrace #Black is to be brave.

#Black is absolute, it is a paradox defined in the ways of all.

I am...

#Black, beautiful and deep.

The balance, the bold, and the belief.

Wear it proudly fear it none.

We are all #Black, we are all one.

# Coppola

Here and now, this moment is perfect.

Perfect in every way I could mean.

I turn inside where my inner sun shines, watching it smile at the one that warms me.

Between this radiance, I am worthy. I am a beam of light.

I am brightness, I illuminate.

I can be seen and felt across the infinite.

It is here and it is now I know.

Confirmed by the inner grace that is I.

I am alive, I am beautiful, and I am a powerful force of being.

I say yes to this moment.

Free falling into the arms of light.

Here and now, I have finally become one, one with time, one with love and most importantly…one with me.

Chapter 5: Wisdom

# Courtship

Life is a poem God is currently reciting to the universe, and we are but a period in its masterpiece.

A point on vast page between and endless number of pages and God must keep writing because there aren't enough words to describe just how amazing she is.

# The Ship of Theseus

I set sail across the vastness of time.

Body be thy vessel as ocean be thy sand.

Who am I?

Child, woman or man?

Anchored by the memories of me,

past be thy scripture as today be thy only word.

Do I feel it?

Acrylic visage smeared into the absurd?

Taken upon the empty canvas of the sea.

Distance be thy voyage as mirage be thy company.

What am I, if not one and the same?

I come from pieces but what peace shall come from me?

Fall away from me, pull me into your depths.

Nothing be thy everything as everything be thy mark.

Take all of me, down to the final nail in plank.

Reveal this ships identity, reveal to me that I am...I am blank.

# Between Fear and Courage

I am pressed against a wall that won't give.

Before me is lion's mane with the eyes to feed.

Helpless not, I know what I must do but in doing I feel as though I maim myself.

Tortuous this act, a litany of hurt rather avoided.

Do I will myself forward or succumb to hollow bones?

The beasts paw depresses unsteady sand and I nauseated with raised and ready hands.

"*Lower your fists and come away with me,*" say whispers of such sweet sleep, speaking ease.

A gentle breeze carried away from what ails.

"*Slip into the void, better death than to fail.*"

The beasts belly rumbles and teeth glint in shadow.

All of me wishes to collapse under such weight but the same weight I bare keeps me there.

Planted like timber, splintered but unbuckling.

I step from the wall that won't give.

Empty palms clasp and grab for my return.

Tempting its embrace, I ponder it.

Fain absence instead of race, pretend as though I never had a place?

Heated breath now beats against my sweaty brow.

Helpless not, I know what I must do.

My shaken heart drums with fury and my nerves twist needles into open pores.

*"I am with you,"* a different voice beckons and I now pressing forward.

Angst my inertia, discomfort my fuel.

Fear was the doing of not and the unease of doing so was my muse.

What I feared most was my own courage, becoming the lion before me.

Now I know; press forward into the pain, because greatness implores ye.

## Chapter 5: Wisdom

# We Are the Voices of Mice and Men

I am one man standing on a lone pillar of truth.

Before me is the world I once knew but know no more.

The sky has been set ablaze as bursts ring out amongst the ruby clouds.

Our air can be seen with the naked eye from soot and ashes blend.

Rubble of then structures, layer in place of earth's crust.

A once steady land trembles now and not from quake, but of war waged between man.

"**Revolution!**"

We cried revolution when injustice became law and they slaughtered our rights.

Race and religion receded, color and creed condemned.

People are now controlled as cattle, and we permitted such sin.

Those we called leaders and blessed with our faith, frowned upon us, declaring themselves our gods and toyed with our fate.

These soulless fallacies thirsted for an unquenchable thing.

Making attempt after attempt to fill a chalice full of power by conquering.

Their eyes emblazoned, our flesh eaten by thunderous whip.

But despite baring blow after blow, we stayed silent.

Muttering these travesties to ourselves, too afraid of the eagle's iron grip.

We feared the silver talons, fangs of wild dogs and unsympathetic beasts.

Others joined the evil dinner party and took part in its feasts.

They willingly swallowed the feces, their words now only worth their weight in waste.

My people were slowly dying under the thumbnail of their governing.

Becoming civilized was another cute phrase for slavery and our tolerance was just a contractual agreement for them to continue their depravity.

"**Revolution**!"

We cried revolution and tears swept the streets with fury.

Man bonded with animal shouting…*"I'd rather be a savage and live amongst the trees if that meant I could have my freedom!"*

Hand embraced hand gripped so tight each could feel the other's heartbeat.

The grounds swelled beneath our feet, as we marched together openly confronting death's door.

Then, with sudden flash hailed alongside screams, the first shot sang its song and the land I once pledged allegiance to, ran thick with rivers red.

Brother beat brother as sister slay sister, leaving me to wonder how did it come to this?

What path was preceded upon in order to invite the apocalypse before Gabriel's horn?

A lasting question as I stand atop this lone pillar of truth against the final frontier of rebellion.

I contemplate the past before I see my journey's end and I find humor here, a great irony, the darkest of jokes.

So, this is a message from the nearing future, from an existence that should not have been.

When your freedoms have been obstructed or you see cruelty and injustice towards your fellow man.

Fight back, stand your ground and say...we are the voices of mice and men!

Chapter 5: Wisdom

# Children of the Yard

Children of the yard!

Point your fingers and laugh; laugh at the men who say they rule you, the men who hold tight to what little power they believe they have.

Laugh at these bullies who are slaves to their wealth and at any man who'd take the role of king. And I ask of thee; who are the true kings and queens?

I say; it is we the people.

The people were forced out of society and robbed by thieves in studded robes.

I say; it is the people who were left in the dark and presumably couldn't fend for their own.

As it turns out, we do not need them.

Their fortunes or their gold.

We do not need them.

Their governing or their control.

We do not need them because we are more than these things!

We are more than these ideals, we are people, not machines.

Therefore, children of the yard, fear not these monsters.

Fear not these men who claim to be gods.

They are not gods, they are clowns!

Take finger and point them out and feel free to laugh. Because under their tyranny and such pains they deal, that laugh may be the last glint of hope found in smile, the last tiny spark of light in blanket darkness, or the final will to find subtle joy although all else is the other.

Children of the yard, this life belongs to us!

So, point your fingers, face your death and laugh at these men who believe they can cease our frolic and stop our play.

Children of the yard, listen to me when I say, today is, and will always be, our day.

Chapter 5: Wisdom

# The Paradox of Imperfection and Perfection

Perfection is imperfection.

A precise equation written in paradox, equating to all and everything around.

Circular in reason, thereby the circle of life.

It is the building blocks of our infinity.

Dueling meanings married as one.

The perfect stage set in an imperfect place.

It is true that nothing in this bountiful universe is perfect, except that everything has an imperfection, thus being absolute perfection.

How madly genius yet divinely wise, that we seek perfection just beyond crystal eyes.

When from inner depths to vision of sight, imperfection flaunts its truth displayed in plain light.

Be ashamed not by flaws, for all is flawed.

Even the very idea of creation.

For if all were truly perfect, the concept of a creator would be unnecessary.

Thus, creation would create itself.

However, we cannot exist without being created and what we create cannot exist without us.

So, embrace what flaws ail you because all is perfect, in that all is imperfect.

We are born and we die.

No different from stars in nebulae, who, through time burn out in the expanse of space.

Or great galaxies that fade as their many hearts vanish.

Even death itself is not perfect, stars leave behind a remnant, as do we in offspring, so do we in memory.

Imperfection is everywhere, no surface is truly smooth, as nothing is truly solid.

Perception of eye fooled by the limits of mind.

Mind in which we do not control, for our minds control us.

Without mind, we do not function, but without us, mind cannot exist.

Therefore, we are imperfect however perfect all the same.

Dizzying this paradox, a dynamic so profound.

Profound in that even this paradox is imperfect, therefore, perfect and I astound.

We are perfect beings living a perfect life.

Crafted as equals, we live and experience, joys of days wrought with sunlight and pain of hardships seething wounds.

Helplessly connected together in a single web.

From the largest of objects to the most microscopic of infinitesimal things.

We are perfectly imperfect, and I wouldn't want it any other way, because this is perfection; we were imperfectly made that way.

# *We Are in This Together*

Until death do us part and unite us again.

Mine...iris in eyes will be eyes wide open.

Trying and failing.

Bleeding, sweating, crying...loving and laughing.

I am quiet in the chaos.

Calm in the collapse.

Always watching, always learning, seeing and listening.

I am here, I am now.

On a journey towards the sun.

Run with me, let us be swept away in its heat together.

Together as one in the only race that matters.

The human one.

Chapter 5: Wisdom

# *Every Death Is a SuperNova*

There...in the void, there is only me.

I...I being the very void, the very void around me.

Ego still, egocentric this centrism feels as my only vessel dies, the only vessel I have connected to all that is real.

Real...what is real?

Am I?

Was I?

Who am I but further.

Some unknown distance further into the void and then...

A silent flash of light.

Its expanse intertwining its fingertips with what I perceive as my own.

Wrapping its warm hands around the emptiness of my own.

I am pulled into it, there is nowhere I can go.

But I am okay because I know that I am home.

Enveloped by this brilliance, false breath knocked out of me.

It is here in the heart of me, I see it now...it is mercy.

## Chapter 5: Wisdom

# The Man with Many Arms

The man with many arms was not always that way, he began with no arms and no hands.

He had no desires and no plans.

It wasn't until he came across a dream and it was blue.

Then two arms were sculpted; molded for him to hold firm to that dream and hold he did.

It was all he knew; his entire sky became blue.

Until one day there came another, and it was green.

The man snatched it from the towering tree without thinking.

In one arm the man held blue and in the other he held green.

Two dreams before him, two dreams it would seem.

Not long after yellow came with red.

So, two more arms were sculpted, molded for him to hold firm to those dreams, and hold he did.

The man with many arms could do it all.

His talents were known greatly big and small.

Then one day in strolled purple.

The man's eyes lit up and his mind raced in circles.

But he already had four limbs, and each were full.

So, he released blue and he watched it vanish from his view.

But the man with many arms would eventually be torn apart.

He couldn't hold on any longer when he realized the only dream that mattered, was his dream from the start and its color was blue.

# Power of Mind, Power of Us

The idea of force and control is a myth.

I am my mind, not my body and my mind is a force acting upon choice, not a choice being forced upon it.

These words do not pertain to me, for only I can force and control me.

Somewhere along the fractures of history, power became an obsession.

This hunger craved wanting and wanting craved more of this hunger.

Each cannibalized the other until their bellies ripped from their plunder and the powers that be, led others to believe; that if any should disagree, that they could control and force themselves upon thee.

I am here to say that this has always been a fallacy.

You see, my hand is of my own and if it were taken in palm of another and forced to touch a cinder hot stove; juxtaposed to reality, I, my realest self never did such a thing.

Because my mind was distant, my mind did not submit.

The powers that be cannot control me if my mind does not commit.

Wicked red, the stage for war was set.

Those who consciously breathe against those who want to control your breath.

But, how can they?

These words are equations without solutions, a philosophy without substance.

Despite a person's persevering effort, they can never change your inner oneness.

The more they try, the more friction they create.

A friction that can become the fire they cannot mitigate. The power of mind and the power of us.

It is greater than the serpent's curse, much deeper than our flesh.

Our truest selves cannot be measured by the beating in our chest.

The idea of force and control is a myth because how could you do either if I myself don't exist?

*Chapter 5: Wisdom*

# My Future Son Asks

My son of future asked me of now, "*what makes a man a man?*"

If I were to speak, my truth would be ill, for I myself did not know the answer.

Steadfast I am to the mirror before me.

Into mine, these pupils I travel freely, hearing voice of youth pose question of grown suits, "*what makes a man a man?*"

Hercules my boy, a man is big and strong!

Muscles like mountains and strength of Greek gods.

Then from mine, these pupils speak, the mirror reflects back someone, not a God...not even Greek.

I am no Hercules, nor have muscles massive of rock.

But I have courage, I am brave.

Lives I am unafraid to save.

A man must fight but my reflection shows love.

A man must be cold, but my reflection shows warmth.

So, a man must be...no.

A man should be...wait...I got it!

A man must be the greatest that he can be, right?

I then ask the mirror; what makes a man a man?

Out of mine, these pupils reflect back, first my iris; I see my eyes.

Then my nose, then my lips and my face.

I see my chest, I see my stomach, my body and all.

Now I see what makes a man a man.

I do...me and whatever I dream to be.

I am a man...I am...me.

Chapter 5: Wisdom

# Forged in Fire

A good man is not born.

Not by chance nor seven breaths upon seven dice.

A good man beareth not from luck's womb.

His birth, not a product by roll or fulfillment of prophecy.

A good man is forged, handcrafted against anvil and hammer.

Molten and burning, he is the dream of a blacksmith.

He is struck by the thunderous pain of his years.

Searing with heat, his defeats will shape him.

Against stacking odds, he will be placed upon the grinding wheel and sharpened.

Then chilled by falling rain, a cloud of his own tears and like stone, he'll harden.

I say, from fire and brimstone, from blood and from water.

A good man is conceived in the dark and from the ashes, fashions himself into light.

A good man is nurtured by the teat of nature.

Neither gentle nor harsh, a good man is designed by mother's hand.

A sword for flesh or a sword for the land, a good man you stand.

Waiver not from your heart, wading amidst trials, you are still true.

Striking not with intent to maim, you inspire.

For, good men maybe fashioned, but they rarely choose to rise.

You are a good man, hope glints within your eyes.

It is not a coincidence; I believe not in happenstance because it takes good men to choose their heroic paths.

A good man is no accident, no fortune or fluke.

A good man is a choice and that good man is you.

*Dedicated to*

*~ My Father*

# My Gift

Born without my consent, starting out in life with an empty mind, my visions were not yet clear.

My life had just begun, but my reasons for living, my purpose, my destiny, had already been written.

My path was already paved and I, chosen to fulfill it.

This is my gift given to me, stowed upon a soul driven to take place with kings above.

My gift is something I have, and it belongs to me.

It's a talent I possess, and I do it best.

Rivals are enemies, but I pay them no attention.

We do not follow aligned or parallel dimensions.

My gift carries with it my future, currently laid to rest, but in time will awaken.

My destiny calls me.

Under providence, I'll succeed, and once my gift is perfected, I will be ready to lead.

My gift, my heart, mind, body, and soul will take me far beyond space into the heaven where nirvana goes.

I know I will be great; my lifetime will be tested.

However, this is my gift; I do it best and will not be bested.

*Chapter 5: Wisdom*

# Wade's Ozymandias

Amidst a sea of sand, peak the remains of two legs.

These pillars break the thin layer of decay from former giants and now it is here trillions of mammoths lay.

For mountains of such grandeur fail to stand against the test of time, but from ankle to knee it lingers towering above divine.

No longer do they support any man.

He has fallen.

He has been swallowed by the land, lost in the expanse of an hourglass, watching as all he ever was crumbles.

Slowly the man may die, yet his legacy carries forward.

All he ever was might vanish, but his mark has become one with the soil.

Erased in heartbeat, his eyes coldly stare half faced into fate.

Whispers of past return, echoing across ages speaking the name, Ozymandias, King of Kings, ancient in poetry screaming.

Know what happened here.

Know of my life.

Know what only the desert will ever know.

That amidst a sea of sand, where rock flows like water, through time and giant stone of dust, from its depths, I stand.

## Chapter 5: Wisdom

# *Starting Again*

I was filling an empty mind, but my mind was entwined with two hands.

Two hands craving to carve out my world and leave me lost in a dark desolate universe.

Oh, and carve they did, all that work to fill my head, deleted and erased from memory.

I was starting again, starting from scratch without instructions for building this complex work of art.

I mean, how can I rewrite a book verbatim if the book vanished without its copy?

How can I repaint a painting precisely if the vision went askew?

What was done before cannot be done the same again, but still, my mind fills and flows with these words and visions.

Down my arms, into my wrist and out my fingertips, out to the device I wield upon the canvas I spill.

Dreams never lost, only corrupted by lost emotions.

Through clutter and trash, I find a needle in the stack, setting fire to the hay and burning it away, leaving only the needle to stay.

Yes...I am starting again.

To be better than I was before.

Arrive to the summit upon my own mountain I climbed.

Here, I will build a new.

Grow from the ashes, like a flower blossoming from soil.
I will be reborn and lushes, all from starting again.

## Chapter 5: Wisdom

# *Mankind Was Given*

Mankind was given five senses to connect with the world, most importantly each other.

Mankind was given intellect to empathize with the world, most importantly each other.

Yet, today I see men who feel not a thing, not unless it is a sweater woven in hate spun from their own string.

They cannot taste, except for the bitter and the taint.

What is sweet is only the foul they speak through their teeth.

Men who cannot smell, except themselves, for their own stench is what they revel in.

Completely deaf by ear, they hear only what they wish to hear, purposely drowning out noises that for them are unfamiliar and unclear.

Men who are blind, more settled in their own darkness, too afraid to see the brilliance of color in a world created through love.

With intellect, man formed ego and ego birthed selfishness.

Leaving connection to starve and empathy to vanish.

Death became the answer, while faith was placed in things of lavish.

Leaving the men of today empty soulless machines, swallowed by the jaws of greed.

Today we can change, open our eyes and see.

This life beats of infinite rhythms, not just you or me.

With intellect came love and so mankind was given heart.

Followed by eyes to see flesh and the mind to perceive its art.

We were given a mouth to speak love and ears to receive it.

Turn away from the calamity and let your soul fully perceive it.

Mankind was given love because together we are free, we were not given freedom because that takes you and me.

## Chapter 5: Wisdom

# *Conformity*

A soul is a being with life, a life that is fair to none.

Yet, there in front of me stands a life, a life that remains peaceful despite the outcome.

I gander at its beauty and envy its strength.

I soak up its knowledge and wisdom with great weight.

I inhale its health, purest of oxygen.

My body with its fortitude toughens.

However, no matter how hard I try, I don't compare.

I don't stand a chance against the towering lumber resting there.

I admire this tree.

I learned to love its entire family.

Trees are my favorite souls because they endure most of all.

Whether it's raining or snowing, twisters or hurricanes blowing.

Mudslides, floods, drought and fires burning.

Trees conform and grow.

They don't cry, complain, nor give up.

Only conform to their space without a single hiccup.

Remaining rooted and conforming to life as it changes.

Silence is not silent; they are speaking their own language.

I wish I could be as sturdy, enduring all there is to endure.

Trees are the most remarkable beings and we overlook their splendor.

Like them, I am stationary, surviving any situation, embracing the wind battering me despite which way I'm facing.

I now understand as trees do, that this universe is much bigger than me.

So, I am grateful for the ground I'm growing in, I am grateful for the trees that be.

Chapter 5: Wisdom

# Essence of Time

There is an essence of time fluttering amongst the air in front of me and I have not slept in the weeks which have passed behind.

Sleeping I won't, the sweet essence of time keeps me awake.

It is beautiful, tantalizing, across the bridge between future and past, now and then.

Always alive and breathing, draining me into exhaustion.

Be it ever so subtle, all I can do is dream.

Falling through fractions of fractures within fractals.

Eyes closed while wide open gates of black pools expand, then drop into eternity following clocks into the distance.

I am pulled along this essence, held by the sheer scent of time's musk.

Half awake, living dead asleep, with eyes wide open as the fragrance of time faints.

Dispelled from such magic, I lose track of the path I began.

I am anxious, this essence counting down what time is left of me, left of the illusionary artist within the conscious me.

I can hear it within the essence of thought, feel it within the essence of touch, taste it within in the essence of food and see it throughout the essence of my life.

Time is of this essence and we are all the essence of time and like everything trapped within its rose-colored diagram, it is just a concept of our minds.

## Chapter 5: Wisdom

# *As the Dominoes Fall*

Life is like an infinite set of dominoes stacked in a tight cluster of rows.

Each with a different appeal, not one brick has an identical seal.

Then, man was given the ability of choice, the right to exercise his many thoughts, opinions, and voice.

Confused and unsure what to do, another sound echoed out.

It addressed itself to you saying, *"make a decision, push the chip over and watch what the cascade results in forward."*

In time, more personalities appeared.

All with their own credence's, some sane and some weird.

Domino after domino fell, creating a chain event that swelled.

Row after row colliding with each other, some columns flipped, twisted and blended with another.

Infinite events started to arise, pushing that domino meant we were to begin our lives.

Life driven in advance because of all our directions.

Once put in motion, there's no stopping its inflections.

The chips will collapse and fall as they may, triggering the next chain of events to come our way.

Good or bad, the story is written by the culmination of solo visions, life beckoning for us to make our collective decisions.

Where will we end up, it's not for any one man to call.

Our lives are in the hands of bones, only as the dominoes fall.

*~Dedicated to*

*Granddaddy*

*Chapter 5: Wisdom*

# When They Say "Impossible"

When they say, "*impossible,*" it is because there is so much unknown.

It becomes the only plausible answer when one cannot provide an answer.

Uncertainty of such mysteries and unforeseeable future, is closed off by the closed minded for fear of farthest truth.

There was once a man of magnificent imagination, who for once couldn't conceive an idea in imagining.

He proclaims the idea is impossible, that if his magnificent mind cannot conceive it, then it must be completely improbable.

Impossibilities are only as powerful as one's mind can fathom.

Residing in the compounds of answerless equations or harden giants that refuse to be defeated.

So, in horror from the coming fight, these men took flight and fleeted.

Afraid to admit facts in the unknowns of nature.

They refused to embrace the sheer scale of possibilities, because the number of infinities, in its ideal of infinite, is far too monolithic for mere thinkers in simplistic.

Negative words are like blindfolds, darker than night.

Blinding the weak until lost in the depths of anonymous.

Nothing is impossible, except for the idea of impossibilities.

Opening a paradox of treasures, another key to a box of infinite possibilities.

The measure of what can be achieved in this expanse we call home is up to us and our minds to find the answers to the unknowns.

For when they say *"impossible,"* know that it's untrue, because if you break the word apart it becomes, *"I'm possible"* and that's true.

## Chapter 5: Wisdom

# Good and Evil Illusions

Without the human element what discerns between what is good from what is bad?

Hero versus villain?

Perhaps a judge's verdict or opinion?

Maybe it's biblical in nature, clear cut, black and white.

However, villains can be hero's and heroes can be villains.

A cycle of circular yin and yang, sin and saved.

Thou shall not judge because everyone is misbehaved.

Good and evil illusions, the truth smeared behind a foggy mirror.

Would this scheme remain present if I could see the whole picture?

Probably not.

So, I don't play God because I'll probably get caught.

Good is good because we determine it so but bad is bad for the same reasoning though.

Then what is justice, if nothing more than a bias view from our ego's eyes?

Is it good or bad that I am living a lie?

A lie based on a truth, cause and effect.

A balanced equinox, birth and death.

Good provoking evil, evil provoking good, the engine driving this dream of illusions and we are under the hood.

## Chapter 5: Wisdom

# Candle Lights

Designed to hold a flame, we were molded with purpose.

Sparked out from darkness, our wicks found the horizon.

Rising above the clout of shadow, our wicks burned brightly.

Sparked from the end of a match, we pushed obscurity back.

Ember by ember, we brought more light into this life. Marveling at such lights we left blazing in the skies.

As time stretched, eyes would dilate, deviating from stars with nothing to remind us of our flame and who we truly are.

Supernatural beings, guardians of love and the force that governs all things.

We are the candlelight, representing sight in shrouded room.

Darkness may be ever consuming, but light is always its tomb. From womb, we were made of wax, flexible yet sturdy, all with a fire burning inside of us, dancing atop stem.

Yet be warned, the wind blows to snuff out these blazes.

A bonfire too big will wipe out darkness throughout ages.

So, we must acknowledge we are the same as common man,

built from wax, flexible yet sturdy, lit with an inferno of might.

Unite as we once were, defending love from darkness, as children in candlelight.

Chapter 5: Wisdom

# *Material Things*

I am sick and tired of wanting things.

Annoyed by preachers and profits promoting coveting.

Promising that in order to obtain, one should be a good person of good energy and thoughts.

Pretty much teaching love is only worth sharing if rewarded, which in layman's terms means, "doggie gets a treat if he sits."

It angers me that so much of mankind has fallen from humbleness, seeking items in attempts of fulfilling their happiness.

Believing the only way to receiving is walking around feeling entitled, spending days and nights focused solely on an object.

Practically placing the outwards, over self, adrift in the dreary desires of products.

Taught that negative emotions are of evil constructs and to feel and express them will only manifest seething pain.

So, now people bury it deep, masking it with fake goods and fake deeds.

Completely desperate to garner what they think they need.

I am sick and tired of wanting things.

Buying and buying and wondering why I still feel this need to cry.

Confused by filling this void with green but still envious of other jubilant human beings.

So, I purchase, and I purchase, chasing an idea that is now a dream.

That my life will be fulfilled through wanting more and more things.

When in truth, I'd be much happier with having absolutely nothing.

Because unless I can smile all alone and appreciate my body, the greatest possession I'll ever own.

Nothing else will truly bring me joy.

I want to be a good person for the sake of being a good person.

Share the arms of love without any notion of expectation.

## Chapter 5: Wisdom

Be content with the air I breathe, the water I intake and the soul I inhabit.

Understanding that anything else is a gift presented to me as a temporary necessity, or in other words, a blessing.

I am sick and tired of wanting things, when I already have everything I need...me, myself and I.

# The Hardest Thing to Do

The hardest part of life is letting go.

So, hands tightly grip loose handles called life, lessening their latch as they climb.

With the intention to grab another and then wonder; how far the climb?

One hand over the other, what a layered path I scale.

What a disjointed ladder I rise, it could all be so easy if I just...I can't!

What nonsense this thought, how negative my claim.

The direction in which I go doesn't matter, what matters is I stay.

I stay tied to it.

Bound to this rock face the human race is obsessed with conquering.

Obsessed with enslaving while ironically enslaving themselves.

Meanwhile, I am longing.

Longing for a better day, a different day.

## Chapter 5: Wisdom

A day easy enough to be had, I just have to...honestly, I've never tripped on LSD, but I question if this world is real.

Often thinking I'm asleep and that maybe I never woke.

Maybe I haven't spoke because I am trapped, trapped inexplicably somewhere in my mind.

Holding onto me, a me that hasn't been me in quite some time.

But who am I but no one?

Just alone one, scaling this fabrication of happiness.

Going on knowing, that what I seek does not rest at the peak.

However, I still find myself stuck, afraid to do what must be done because the hardest part of life is letting go and freedom is in the falling.

# Images on Fire

Beauty burns.

It is a fire placed on flesh, eating away the youth beneath.

Every day that passes we mourn the death of our younger self.

Every hour, every minute and every second, we wilt.

Petals falling from sweltering skies, combusting into flames before their beauty can be held.

How foolish to give life's purpose to something fleeting.

Placing value in a dying portrait.

A body frozen, vulnerable to father's light.

Icarus burned the way we are burning.

Ice is the flesh; it is solid, but it is cold, and it is brittle.

Yet, hubris keeps us blind to illusions of perfection.

Towards the flame, our ice sculptures frolic.

Tracing the timeline that has been drawn before.

Images on fire now melting away, leaving the soul with nothing but ashes of old age.

*Chapter 5: Wisdom*

# *Everything Happens and There Is A Reason*

At this very moment, you made a choice and in a matter of minutes, you will have made several. Sculpting a sculpture of future or painting vibrantly of the present.

Everything happens and there is a reason.

We may think we know it, but we don't.

For the occurrence of an event caused by self-choosing could be meant for that gentleman you've never met.

Every step is a ripple in a calm lake, expanding out into the quantum.

Ricocheting off the tops of atoms and quarks, bouncing around moment to moment, second to second, shifting with the current of air and water, waking an event to happen with reason.

Death might transpire, molding more melancholy.

Hurt could result, creating caverns of cuts.

Yet in principle, such ache is temporary and the abusive love between good and bad a necessary. Projecting life in a forward motion like bullet from pistol, accelerating faster than song can be heard.

Gazelle giving birth and predator devouring prey, everything happens and there is a reason. Circular and sound we spin in this beautiful playground, tied together in unity based upon the choices we make in this web.

Trying to grasp a vision of God deeper than comprehension as we propel towards divinity and a greater ascension.

I may not understand causality in the episode at hand, but I do know it all plays a part in an incomplete plan.

That every frown and every grin, every miracle and every sin, everything happens for a reason, but it is up to us to find the good in that reason.

*Chapter 5: Wisdom*

# Destiny Is Known in Silence

The moment comes and all is still, except the road you walk which bends and at times breaks. Conquering balance tilting on the edge of an empty cup, filled by undying thirst for more, more being, more life, more you,

playing at this game of improvisation, switching between lives.

Sometimes forgetting the difference between it and your own.

Lost in the land of middle, feeling alive, seeing the unseen, living the dream, arriving, standing firm atop swaying wires, undeterred by fear.

The moment comes and all is still, except the road you walk which bends and at times, it breaks.

Shifting in vibrations, loud sounds expand the air in instruments bellowing.

Hands of a clock moving forward while angels wait in anticipation, jumping and screaming in the back of your mind, waiting for a choice, epic in sense, fate is at hand.

For no trumpets sound when the significant decisions in our lives are made.

Destiny is made known quietly amongst the concaves of our souls.

Chapter 5: Wisdom

# *Our Digital World*

With one click of a mouse, I am transported home.

Through a vast network of invisible circuits, I live in another zone.

I flow through tubular structures, gateways to galaxies and planets beyond.

With one click of a mouse I can swim in many ponds. Some big, some small, some naughty and some nice.

Transfixed in gaze, I stare into my L.E.D all night.

Until sunrise arrives, beaming with ultraviolet rays.

Then I pull out my phone, become transfixed and begin my day.

With one push of a button I can pull many angry birds out of a hat and like magic, I can prove any fact. I'll always have an answer, just ask the question, *"why*?"

Wait...hold on a sec...I got a text...it reads, *"Lol hi."*

I can visit alien worlds comfortable in my abode or on the go.

Living in the matrix twenty-four seven is all I know.

Hold on a sec...I gotta charge my phone. I can't live without it; I feel so alone.

With one click of a mouse, I am transported to a new place.

If I wanted to, I could even disappear without a trace.

btw, muh speling has gotin wrse doh.

u gonna b rotfl when I tex u dis typo.

You can't argue with my followers; biatch, I'm a superstar.

Even posted pictures with a Bentley, although it's not my real car.

With one click of a mouse, I can be anything I desire.

Living as many lives as I wish through ether and wires.

Losing track of time, possibly feeding my addiction.

I wonder if I've developed any of the same symptoms.

For instance, squawking across the sky while, at pigs, you are hurled.

Oh, my lord, I just realized...I'm the one lost in the purgatory of our digital world.

Chapter 5: Wisdom

# *Right Now*

We are the epic moment.

A beat sped up to a singular note.

We are the beginning, the middle, and the end.

The everything that was and will be.

We are the music; we are the one sound.

Resonant and infinite.

We are only and have always been...

Right now.

# Grey

Looking into a mirror, I find a shadow staring back.

It laughs at me; it taunts me and threatens to stuff my life in a tiny sack.

If gone unchecked, I just might do that.

For I am the villain of my own story.

"**Meanwhile**:"

Looking into a mirror, I find a hero staring back.

Pushing me forward, daring me to be great despite the powers I lack.

Believe in me, I am the one to do it.

For I am the hero of my own story.

>We are silver, we are grey, two faces of one coin.
>
>>Hero and villain, one and the same.
>
>Scripture writ in blood wine, a verse as old as time.
>
>>A tale about choices, a story uniquely mine.

*Chapter 5: Wisdom*

# Reincarnation

So much time will pass.

Every conceivable arrangement of atoms will be had.

Countless configurations of reality will play.

Not even an infinite amount of time can fathom.

And so...with much, much time.

I will be born again.

I will live, I will love, I will lose.

I will be.

From the ashes, I will rise.

Faster than death can reopen its eyes.

I will push from mother's womb and fall into gentle cradle.

**Deja vu.**

# Schrödinger's Cat

We are.

We have always been but never were to begin with.

I am dead.

I have always been dead but somehow, I am still dying.

This is real.

It has always been real but somehow just a dream.

A dream, dreamt by a dreamer, dreamt by a dreamer and so on...dreaming of dreamers dreaming.

A possibility probable until the dreamer looks in the box.

## The All

This, that and the other...

I am the Devil.

I am God.

I am the sinner and I am the saint.

Cry in my arms, I am man and I am woman.

I am all time and I am nothing.

I remember lusting and planting seed.

I remember loving and receiving the same.

Break me not for I am already broken.

Live as dust for I am already dead.

There was no beginning and there isn't an end.

Only what is and what has always been.

I am All and you are me.

Death is God and soon you'll see.

A moment not, through eyes can be.

All exists because we are free.

# Way Back

I want you to know that I know you.

We go back...*waaay* back, remember?

I only know because I see the **ALL** in you.

The same **ALL** I see in me too.

Absent of everything but the space in between.

The paper everything is drawn upon, the connection between **ALL** things.

You see?

I know you and you know me too.

We know everything and everybody, we just don't know we do.

Find the **ALL** within yourself, see what can't be unseen.

Let someone else know that you know them, this is the *Great Remembering*.

*Chapter 5: Wisdom*

# The Result of Holding On

Holding onto yesterday and the agony yet to come, will create sorrow, a sore, which can grow and overrun.

Colliding into surface like comet, ejecting soot into air, blackening lungs as if it were a cigarette's affair.

Calling it "*our precious*," we act like lords over rings, but such things deteriorate a soul until we are unworthy kings.

Hoarding emotions, secrets and items, we become a slave to lies, eventually lying alone in the cold, finding solace as we die.

But death should not be a resort to our freedom, liberation from the chains we lock ourselves in should be the reason.

Finding a way of releasing meaningless things from being, opening eyes to only truth, awakening and finally seeing.

The result of holding on has the same meaning as prison, and life bountiful with energy has only one primary mission.

Freedom and the will to roam free, living and existing abundantly.

To hold onto anything is ill attempt to imprison this energy, but like an explosion, you cannot contain this entity.

Words with such power, if not spoken, can rot without sympathy, emotions if not released can devour a man internally.

Something as simple as rock can release enough force to become a diamond sparkling.

Holding onto the dirt will only further ones darkening.

If it is joy, share it with the world and the world will embrace it.

If it is pain, expel it from the body and the world will extinguish it.

Relinquish yourself, pride and fear to the world and be amazed at what she'll show.

That peace, love, and harmony can come, if everyone would start letting go.

*Chapter 5: Wisdom*

# Dipped in Gold

I woke today, dipped in gold.

Bold and brilliant, I under the morning star saw genius in design.

Sons die, while stars give birth to gold and when gold gives birth to life, the "L" slips away leaving traces of God in its wake.

Follow it now.

Deep into the abyss, deep into that quiet night.

Carry it with you and fear not.

You awoke this morning dipped in Gold.

Like me, you were born shimmering and shining, bathed in divine light, delivered from a burning heart.

Collectively, we are precious metals.

Literally, worth our weight in gold.

Priceless, becoming all the more sacred with each rising sun.

We woke this day, dipped in gold.

Beautiful, stunning, we are kings and queens united under the honey glaze of glory.

So, I gaze and marvel at the golden glow of gold all around.

Today I woke as you have, dipped in gold.

Sons will die and suns will rise, and the sons that rise know,

true wealth lay within.

Chapter 5: Wisdom

# The Scope of Blackness

Hear ye I say, listen as I speaketh truth.

I...am a black man with black eyes.

Born with black roots and black shoots.

Turn off the lights?

No need. Because I'm the **BLACKEST** proof.

Black is good...Oh, so good and black is bad...at times, very bad.

In fact, black. Black is everything to be had.

It is more than a color, it's a concept and when the scope of blackness is applied to people it becomes...complex.

Like, righteous men of color who dawn their beautiful black suit and wear it with shame.

Or lash out, killing other righteous men of color because of internal hurt and misplaced pain.

Brilliant black knights lost in the complexities of a black night.

No stars, no guiding light. Only hope and this instinctual will to fight on.

Because today, our black brothers are in need of father figures or at least a figure more father some than their own and a decent home.

Not a roof over your head.

I'm talking about a body you haven't been made to believe is evil.

A temple worthy of worship because blackness (close your eyes) it is the very quintessence of peaceful.

And there are those who know this.

I have seen it with my own eyes.

They're black men who wear black crowns for their black kings I surmise.

They understand black beauty, black brilliance, black excellence, and black elegance.

That being black is a burden for black absorbs all things, even light and light is love, thereby making blackness an accumulation of everything.

It is feared because it's the least understood.

## Chapter 5: Wisdom

It is the beginning, the middle and the end, blackness is not where God stood...it's where God stands.

God let there be light, but that light was born from the blackest hands.

So, King among Kings and the silent responsibility of being black.

Hear me true, I speak to you.

Though the weight is heavy, carry it just.

We are Black Kings, living definitions of unconditional love.

Therefore, it's not only a necessity, it's a must.

Wear your black suit and wear it with pride because young brothers you are a Universal guide.

You are complicated and still a beacon, you're a father figure broken and unbroken.

Remember always, you're a concept conceived in the miracle of black.

You are the **BLACKEST KING**, the very essence of **EVERYTHING** and that is the scope of blackness.

# I Run With You

It began with a rhythm, a tour de force of drums and beats.

A people, my family, tribal and unleashed.

The blood of me stamped their feet around a fire baited by the winds of time.

Beginning with a fight for survival against a predator on the front line.

Weapons embedded in the palms of shaking grasps, I ran with you.

Into the jaws of a beast, fearing if this shall be our last, I ran with you.

Our battle cries from the cross, echoes of a solemn vow.

Brother, I ran with you then, and I run with you, right now.

It continued on a foreign land, a baby ripped from the arms of its parents.

A people, my family, whipped and worked into the arms of perseverance.

## Chapter 5: Wisdom

The blood of me stamped their feet across the jagged terrain of freedom.

In search for answers, perhaps... even a God-given reason.

Soles coarse, blistered and bled, I ran with you.

From beasts who stained our peace with red, I ran with you.

Our battle cries from the cross, echoes of a solemn vow.

Brother, I ran with you then, and I run with you, right now.

It didn't end with a war, the sound of drums are now bodies beating against tree trunks.

A people, my family, segregated, separated and treated worse than street junk.

The blood of me stamped their feet between the fine lines of color and life.

Exposing chaos in a battle that would decide future tides.

Hand in hand to accomplish a dream, I ran with you.

Even after shots rang out and air filled with screams, I ran with you.

Our battle cries from the cross, echoes of a solemn vow.

Brother, I ran with you then, and I run with you, right now.

Progress, the silent killer of progress.

A people, my family, so much has changed but hatred refuses to come forward and confess.

What a mess, rods beat kings and the color black is publicly crucified.

We all have nice things now, but one is perpetually euthanized.

It's disguised, rigged, and although we knew, I ran with you.

Through the pain, struggle, and despair, I ran with you.

Our battle cries from the cross, echoes of a solemn vow,

Brother, I ran with you then, and I run with you, right now.

It began with a shot, a tour de force of sulfur and fire.

A man, a human being unknowingly running into the arms of an angel's choir.

The blood of me stopped in his tracks, another me, laid firmly on his back.

## Chapter 5: Wisdom

After all this time, still, we fight against the beast's heinous attacks.

The day you left your house, I was running with you.

The moment they shot you down, I was running with you.

Our battle cries from the cross, the echo of a solemn vow.

My brother...my sister...I ran with you then, and I am still running with you, right now.

Not in fear, no, with my head held high.

We've been running towards a brighter day blessed by clearing skies.

Hear our battle cries from the cross, the echoes of a solemn vow.

We ran with our ancestors then and they run with us right now.

Together, always, we are tribe.

# My Poem for the World

Stardust, energy, and life. Liberation from what was nothing came us.

Envisioned, thought and discovered. We were forged from stars.

So, stare we must at our night sky, which glistens, but as they stare back, we shine.

For the world, I say, my brothers and sisters, we share space as one and the same.

Gravity holds us, dreams which freed.

In this world, there is no such thing as me.

For what is can only be; For if what is, is we.

Unity under sun, as its embrace, warms us.

It is love which makes us, as we use love to make life, art, what is now past, what is present and what will be future.

For the world, I say, my brothers and sisters, extend your hands, let any take hold and hold strong to any.

We are bonded through stars and at a time we were one.

## Chapter 5: Wisdom

Obscured by glare, in blindness, hate has no room to grow nor color to judge, yet our energy will forever flow, and this is a message to the world.

Beating heart of beautiful red, orchestral in music and source,

born by mother nurtured seed of man, I say we are human blessed of our motherland.

Her arms remain open to us, as do mine.

I embrace the human race; I embrace all of mankind.

*Inspired by and dedicated to*

*~ Maya Angelou*

BELIEVE IN YOUR DREAMS FOR THEY BELIEVE IN YOU.

THEREFORE IT'S NOT A MATTER OF CAN'T, ONLY WHAT YOU WILL OR WON'T DO.

PUT LOVE IN YOUR HEART AND CARRY IT WITH YOU THROUGH THE DARK.

LET DOUBT AND FEAR KNOW THE MIGHTY COURAGE IN YOUR HEART

AND WHEN THEY SAY YOU'LL FAIL OR YOUR DREAMS ARE NOT PLAUSIBLE,

LOOK THEM IN THEIR EYES AND SAY...

ANYTHING IS POSSIBLE.

# About the Author

Wade F. Wilson was born in Oakland California and like so many, he moved to Los Angeles to pursue his dreams of becoming a professional actor. After graduating California State University of Los Angeles, in 2010, Mr. Wilson dove headfirst into the industry.

He started with writing and directing and ended up producing several original stage pieces. His favorite being "Inside the Mind of Me". Then in 2015, Wade's career blossomed when he landed an opportunity to work with the extraordinary Spike Lee. Wade say's that was the year his life hit an inflection point and changed for the better. Since then, he has had continued success and has been blessed to work on projects he never imagined he could. Mr. Wilson's aspiration goes beyond that of an actor though, and starting with this book, he looks to develop his talents as a poet and a storyteller. He hopes his words will uplift, heal and carry his readers to that higher place we all belong. "Cogito ergo sum."

## Connect with me at...

*Email:* Wealth4rmWisdom@gmail.com